# First World War
## and Army of Occupation
# War Diary
## France, Belgium and Germany

37 DIVISION
63 Infantry Brigade
Prince Albert's (Somerset Light Infantry)
8th Battalion
28 July 1916 - 24 April 1919

WO95/2529/2

The Naval & Military Press Ltd
www.nmarchive.com
**Published in association with The National Archives**

Published by

The Naval & Military Press Ltd

Unit 10 Ridgewood Industrial Park,
Uckfield, East Sussex,
TN22 5QE England
Tel: +44 (0) 1825 749494

www.naval-military-press.com

www.nmarchive.com

*This diary has been reprinted in facsimile from the original. Any imperfections are inevitably reproduced and the quality may fall short of modern type and cartographic standards.*

© **Crown Copyright**
**Images reproduced by permission of The National Archives, London, England, 2015.**

# Contents

| Document type | Place/Title | Date From | Date To |
|---|---|---|---|
| Heading | WO95/2529/2 | | |
| Heading | Reference WO95 2529 8th Bn Somerset Light Infantry Aug 1916-Apr 1919 Conservation Department. | | |
| Heading | 37th Division 63rd Infy Bde 8th Bn Somerset Lt Infy Aug 1916-Apr 1919 From 21 Div. 63 Bde. | | |
| War Diary | Berthonval I | 01/08/1916 | 08/08/1916 |
| War Diary | Berthonval | 06/08/1916 | 09/08/1916 |
| War Diary | Berthonval | 03/08/1916 | 03/08/1916 |
| War Diary | Berthonval | 01/08/1916 | 13/08/1916 |
| War Diary | Berthonval | 28/07/1916 | 28/07/1916 |
| War Diary | Berthonval | 11/08/1916 | 21/08/1916 |
| War Diary | Berthonval | 11/08/1916 | 16/08/1916 |
| War Diary | Berthonval | 14/08/1916 | 19/08/1916 |
| War Diary | Berthonval | 18/08/1916 | 18/08/1916 |
| War Diary | Berthonval | 17/08/1916 | 18/08/1916 |
| War Diary | Berthonval | 11/08/1916 | 23/08/1916 |
| War Diary | Berthonval | 16/08/1916 | 30/08/1916 |
| War Diary | Souchez. I | 02/09/1916 | 03/09/1916 |
| War Diary | Souchez. I | 01/09/1916 | 13/09/1916 |
| War Diary | Souchez. I | 11/09/1916 | 11/09/1916 |
| War Diary | Souchez. I | 09/09/1916 | 21/09/1916 |
| War Diary | Souchez. I | 14/09/1916 | 21/09/1916 |
| War Diary | Souchez. I | 09/09/1916 | 22/09/1916 |
| War Diary | Souchez. I | 16/09/1916 | 27/09/1916 |
| War Diary | Souchez. I | 26/09/1916 | 29/09/1916 |
| War Diary | Souchez. I | 24/09/1916 | 06/10/1916 |
| War Diary | Souchez. II | 12/10/1916 | 16/10/1916 |
| War Diary | Souchez. II | 03/10/1916 | 05/10/1916 |
| War Diary | Souchez. II | 29/09/1916 | 29/09/1916 |
| War Diary | Souchez. II | 07/09/1916 | 27/10/1916 |
| War Diary | Souchez. II | 11/10/1916 | 13/10/1916 |
| War Diary | Souchez. II | 12/10/1916 | 17/10/1916 |
| War Diary | Souchez. II | 24/10/1916 | 25/10/1916 |
| War Diary | Souchez. II | 26/10/1916 | 27/10/1916 |
| War Diary | Souchez. II | 25/10/1916 | 26/10/1916 |
| War Diary | Souchez. II | 16/10/1916 | 26/10/1916 |
| War Diary | Souchez. II | 22/10/1916 | 30/10/1916 |
| Miscellaneous | A Form. Messages And Signals. | | |
| War Diary | | 01/11/1916 | 26/11/1916 |
| War Diary | | 03/11/1916 | 19/11/1916 |
| War Diary | | 14/11/1916 | 14/11/1916 |
| War Diary | | 19/11/1916 | 27/11/1916 |
| War Diary | | 19/11/1916 | 28/11/1916 |
| War Diary | | 05/11/1916 | 29/11/1916 |
| War Diary | | 14/11/1916 | 22/12/1916 |
| War Diary | | 09/12/1916 | 09/12/1916 |
| War Diary | | 01/12/1916 | 10/12/1916 |
| War Diary | | 09/12/1916 | 28/12/1916 |
| War Diary | | 18/12/1916 | 28/12/1916 |
| War Diary | | 27/12/1916 | 30/12/1916 |

| Type | Description | Start | End |
|---|---|---|---|
| War Diary | | 09/12/1916 | 30/12/1916 |
| Heading | War Diary 8 Somersets January 1917 Vol 17 | | |
| War Diary | | 02/01/1917 | 28/01/1917 |
| War Diary | | 25/01/1917 | 25/01/1917 |
| War Diary | | 03/01/1917 | 29/01/1917 |
| War Diary | | 24/01/1917 | 24/01/1917 |
| Heading | War Diary 8th Somerset. L.I. Feb 1917 Vol 18 | | |
| War Diary | | 22/02/1917 | 23/02/1917 |
| War Diary | | 07/02/1917 | 25/02/1917 |
| War Diary | | 01/02/1917 | 25/02/1917 |
| War Diary | | 03/02/1917 | 10/03/1917 |
| War Diary | | 01/03/1917 | 16/03/1917 |
| War Diary | | 10/03/1917 | 30/04/1917 |
| War Diary | | 01/04/1917 | 05/04/1917 |
| War Diary | | 01/04/1917 | 29/04/1917 |
| Miscellaneous | Operations 9th-12th April. | | |
| Miscellaneous | Operations April 22nd. | | |
| Miscellaneous | Operations April 28th 1917 | 28/04/1917 | 28/04/1917 |
| Heading | War Diary 8th Somerset L.I. May 1917 Vol 21 | | |
| War Diary | | 06/05/1917 | 28/05/1917 |
| War Diary | | 11/05/1917 | 31/05/1917 |
| Heading | War Diary 8th Somersets June 1917 Vol 22 | | |
| War Diary | | 01/06/1917 | 29/06/1917 |
| War Diary | | 02/06/1917 | 04/06/1917 |
| War Diary | | 01/06/1917 | 28/06/1917 |
| Heading | War Diary 6th Somersets July 1917 Vol 23 | | |
| War Diary | | 02/07/1917 | 29/07/1917 |
| War Diary | | 03/07/1917 | 13/07/1917 |
| War Diary | | 10/07/1917 | 15/07/1917 |
| War Diary | | 14/07/1917 | 18/07/1917 |
| War Diary | | 17/07/1917 | 20/07/1917 |
| War Diary | | 18/07/1917 | 30/07/1917 |
| Heading | War Diary 8th Somersets Aug 1917 Vol 24 | | |
| War Diary | | 29/07/1917 | 29/08/1917 |
| War Diary | | 31/07/1917 | 31/07/1917 |
| War Diary | | 30/07/1917 | 31/07/1917 |
| War Diary | | 03/08/1917 | 30/08/1917 |
| Heading | War Diary 8th Somersets Sept. 1917 Vol 25 | | |
| War Diary | | 07/09/1917 | 27/09/1917 |
| War Diary | | 01/09/1917 | 26/09/1917 |
| War Diary | | 25/09/1917 | 25/09/1917 |
| Heading | War Diary 8th Somersets Oct 1917 Vol 26 | | |
| War Diary | | 01/10/1917 | 24/10/1917 |
| War Diary | | 05/10/1917 | 29/10/1917 |
| War Diary | War Diary For November 1917 | | |
| War Diary | | 07/12/1917 | 27/12/1917 |
| Heading | 63rd Brigade. 37th Division. 8th Battalion The Somerset Light Infantry. January 1918 | | |
| Miscellaneous | War Diary For January 1918 | | |
| War Diary | | 05/01/1918 | 10/01/1918 |
| War Diary | | 04/01/1918 | 29/01/1918 |
| War Diary | | 25/01/1918 | 26/01/1918 |
| Heading | 63rd Brigade. 37th Division. 8th Battalion The Somerset Light Infantry. February 1918 | | |
| War Diary | | 14/02/1918 | 27/02/1918 |
| War Diary | | 01/02/1918 | 23/02/1918 |

| | | | |
|---|---|---|---|
| War Diary | | 18/02/1918 | 19/02/1918 |
| War Diary | | 12/02/1918 | 26/02/1918 |
| Heading | 63rd Brigade. 37th Division. 8th Battalion The Somerset Light Infantry March 1918 | | |
| War Diary | | 01/03/1918 | 31/03/1918 |
| War Diary | | 03/03/1918 | 14/03/1918 |
| War Diary | | 12/03/1918 | 20/03/1918 |
| War Diary | | 19/03/1918 | 26/03/1918 |
| War Diary | | 24/03/1918 | 27/03/1918 |
| Heading | 63rd Brigade. 37th Division. War Diary 8th Battalion The Somerset Light Infantry April 1918 | | |
| War Diary | | 01/04/1918 | 22/04/1918 |
| War Diary | | 28/03/1918 | 28/03/1918 |
| War Diary | | 07/04/1918 | 12/04/1918 |
| War Diary | | 10/04/1918 | 19/04/1918 |
| War Diary | | 11/04/1918 | 25/04/1918 |
| War Diary | | 11/04/1918 | 26/04/1918 |
| Heading | 63rd Brigade. 37th Division. 8th Battalion The Somerset Light Infantry. May 1918 | | |
| War Diary | | 01/05/1918 | 30/05/1918 |
| War Diary | | 07/05/1918 | 07/05/1918 |
| War Diary | | 01/05/1918 | 09/05/1918 |
| War Diary | | 08/05/1918 | 10/05/1918 |
| War Diary | | 08/05/1918 | 08/05/1918 |
| War Diary | | 07/05/1918 | 11/05/1918 |
| War Diary | | 10/05/1918 | 17/05/1918 |
| War Diary | | 16/05/1918 | 23/05/1918 |
| War Diary | | 22/05/1918 | 27/05/1918 |
| Heading | 63rd Brigade. 37th Division. 8th Battalion The Somerset Light Infantry June 1918 | | |
| War Diary | | 05/06/1918 | 25/06/1918 |
| War Diary | | 23/05/1918 | 24/06/1918 |
| Heading | 63rd Brigade. 37th Division. 8th Battalion The Somerset Light Infantry July 1918 | | |
| War Diary | | 06/07/1918 | 29/07/1918 |
| War Diary | | 08/07/1918 | 29/07/1918 |
| War Diary | | 13/07/1918 | 13/07/1918 |
| Heading | 63rd Brigade. 37th Division. 8th Battalion The Somerset Light Infantry August 1918 | | |
| War Diary | | 05/08/1918 | 26/08/1918 |
| War Diary | | 05/08/1918 | 15/08/1918 |
| War Diary | | 12/08/1918 | 12/08/1918 |
| War Diary | | 10/08/1918 | 12/08/1918 |
| War Diary | | 11/08/1918 | 22/08/1918 |
| War Diary | | 19/08/1918 | 23/08/1918 |
| War Diary | | 18/08/1918 | 26/08/1918 |
| War Diary | | 24/08/1918 | 24/08/1918 |
| War Diary | | 23/08/1918 | 29/08/1918 |
| War Diary | | 27/08/1918 | 31/08/1918 |
| War Diary | | 26/08/1918 | 26/08/1918 |
| War Diary | | 25/08/1918 | 25/08/1918 |
| Miscellaneous | Report On Operations Carried Out By 8th (S) Bn. Somerset Light Infantry. 21st To 26th August 1918 | 21/08/1918 | 21/08/1918 |
| Heading | 63rd Brigade. 37th Division. 8th Battalion The Somerset Light Infantry September 1918 | | |
| War Diary | | 01/09/1918 | 01/09/1918 |

| | | | |
|---|---|---|---|
| War Diary | | 31/08/1918 | 31/08/1918 |
| War Diary | | 01/09/1918 | 06/09/1918 |
| War Diary | | 05/09/1918 | 09/09/1918 |
| War Diary | | 02/09/1918 | 12/09/1918 |
| War Diary | | 09/08/1918 | 13/09/1918 |
| War Diary | | 12/09/1918 | 16/09/1918 |
| War Diary | | 10/09/1918 | 19/09/1918 |
| War Diary | | 15/09/1918 | 23/09/1918 |
| War Diary | | 22/09/1918 | 22/09/1918 |
| War Diary | | 12/09/1918 | 25/09/1918 |
| War Diary | | 11/09/1918 | 29/09/1918 |
| War Diary | | 16/09/1918 | 30/09/1918 |
| War Diary | | 03/09/1918 | 30/09/1918 |
| Miscellaneous | Report On Operations Carried Out By 6th (S) Bn Somerset Light Infantry From 3rd To 11th Sept. 1918 | 03/09/1918 | 03/09/1918 |
| War Diary | To:- O.C. "C" Coy. | 09/09/1918 | 09/09/1918 |
| Miscellaneous | Orders Issued To Companies During Operations 3.9.18 To 11.9.18 | 03/09/1918 | 03/09/1918 |
| Operation(al) Order(s) | Operation Orders No. 24 8th (S) Bn. Somerset Light Infantry. | 07/09/1918 | 07/09/1918 |
| Operation(al) Order(s) | Operation Orders No. 95 8th (S) Bn Somerset Light Infantry | 09/09/1918 | 09/09/1918 |
| Operation(al) Order(s) | Operation Order No. 96 8th (S) Bn Somerset Light Infantry. | 11/09/1918 | 11/09/1918 |
| Miscellaneous | Handing Over Report | 04/09/1918 | 04/09/1918 |
| Map | | | |
| Heading | 63rd Brigade. 37th Division. 8th Battalion The Somerset Light Infantry October 1918 | | |
| War Diary | | 30/09/1918 | 31/10/1918 |
| War Diary | | 02/10/1918 | 10/10/1918 |
| War Diary | | 05/10/1918 | 17/10/1918 |
| War Diary | | 15/10/1918 | 19/10/1918 |
| War Diary | | 18/10/1918 | 31/10/1918 |
| Operation(al) Order(s) | Operation Orders No. X.Z.2. 8th (S) Bn. Somerset Light Infantry. | | |
| Miscellaneous | Report On Minor Operations Carried Out On Night Of 29th/30th October 1918 By 8th Somerset Light Infantry In Conjuction With 1st Bn. N.Z.R.B. | 01/11/1918 | 01/11/1918 |
| Heading | 63rd Brigade. 37th Division. 8th Battalion The Somerset Light Infantry November 1918 | | |
| War Diary | | 01/11/1918 | 26/11/1918 |
| War Diary | | 25/11/1918 | 28/11/1918 |
| War Diary | | 25/11/1918 | 26/11/1918 |
| War Diary | | 02/11/1918 | 04/11/1918 |
| War Diary | | 02/11/1918 | 13/11/1918 |
| War Diary | | 06/11/1918 | 11/11/1918 |
| War Diary | | 09/11/1918 | 13/11/1918 |
| War Diary | | 12/11/1918 | 18/11/1918 |
| War Diary | | 15/11/1918 | 25/11/1918 |
| War Diary | | 23/11/1918 | 29/11/1918 |
| Miscellaneous | Report On Operation For November 4th & 6th 1918 | 04/11/1918 | 04/11/1918 |
| Miscellaneous | My Dear Sheringham. | 05/11/1918 | 05/11/1918 |
| Heading | 63rd Brigade. 37th Division. 8th Battalion The Somerset Light Infantry December 1918 | | |
| War Diary | | 01/12/1918 | 31/12/1918 |
| Miscellaneous | War Diary For December 1918 8th (S) Bn Somerset L.I. | 09/12/1918 | 09/12/1918 |

| | | | |
|---|---|---|---|
| War Diary | | 02/12/1918 | 12/12/1918 |
| War Diary | | 09/12/1918 | 13/12/1918 |
| War Diary | | 12/12/1918 | 12/12/1918 |
| War Diary | | 08/12/1918 | 23/12/1918 |
| War Diary | | 14/12/1918 | 26/12/1918 |
| War Diary | | 24/12/1918 | 25/12/1918 |
| War Diary | | 23/12/1918 | 26/12/1918 |
| War Diary | | 24/12/1918 | 17/01/1919 |
| War Diary | | 16/01/1919 | 21/01/1919 |
| War Diary | | 01/01/1919 | 05/01/1919 |
| War Diary | | 03/01/1919 | 03/01/1919 |
| War Diary | | 27/12/1918 | 20/01/1919 |
| War Diary | | 19/01/1919 | 22/01/1919 |
| War Diary | | 21/01/1919 | 28/02/1919 |
| War Diary | | 04/02/1919 | 27/02/1919 |
| Miscellaneous | Lt. Col. Sir Frederick Ponsonby Bart. St James Palace. London W | 03/02/1919 | 03/02/1919 |
| War Diary | | 02/03/1919 | 31/03/1919 |
| War Diary | | 11/03/1919 | 24/04/1919 |

WO 95
2529/2

**REFERENCE**

**WO**

**95**

**2529**

**8th BN SOMERSET LIGHT INFANTRY AUG 1916 – APR 1919**

CONSERVATION DEPARTMENT

11-3-1999

37TH DIVISION
63RD INFY BDE

8TH BN SOMERSET LT INFY
AUG 1916-APR 1919

FROM 21 DIV 63 BDE

# WAR DIARY
## INTELLIGENCE SUMMARY

Army Form C. 2118

Vol 12

| Place | Date | Hour | Summary of Events and Information | Remarks and references to Appendices |
|---|---|---|---|---|
| Berthonval | 1-8-16 | | Battalion in the trenches "A" & "C" Coys. front line "B" Coy in local support. | Aug 16 |
| | 5-8-16 | | 2nd Lt. D.T. Chaplin Hall joined the Battn. in the trenches. — Date of posting 1/8/16. | Ap 19 |
| | | | 2nd Lt. V.G. Willatt joined the Buffs posted 3/8/16. | |
| | | | 2nd Lt. A.T. Hall notified to had been awarded "Military Cross" "Action July 1916" where all the senior officers of the Battalion had become casualties. He being 2nd/Lt. took command. He gathered all available men and continued the advance. He carried out bombing attacks, and on his own initiative and by his example and courage succeeded in consolidating and holding the position which the Battalion had gained. | |
| | 6-8-16 | | Strafe at 100. O.R. carried from Base — 2nd Lieut Kensford Cyclist Battalion. 2nd Lt. A. Emms went out on his 1st patrol with 8 men (volunteers) with the object of getting a prisoner or identifications. The patrol went out at 11-0 p.m. and returned about 1-30 a.m., not having encountered any enemy. Just as the last man was coming in out the parapet, an enemy party by it possibly showed lines up. The enemy immediately threw on, but without other rifle fire on small torpedoes. They one and held the first to be fired landed in our trench, a direct hit on poor Emms, who was killed instantly. 2 O.R. wounded — one of whom was the sentry on duty, 2nd Lieutenants were serving in ZOUAVE VALLEY. — A cross has been erected over his grave. | |
| | 7-8-16 | | 1. C.R. killed — a private in the Hampstead Regt. attacked. | |

Maitland Hardyman
2nd/4 Bn. Roy.
E.S. Br. Seventh Bat.

# WAR DIARY or INTELLIGENCE SUMMARY

Army Form C. 2118

| Place | Date | Hour | Summary of Events and Information | Remarks and references to Appendices |
|---|---|---|---|---|
| Berthonval | 7.8.16 | | 2nd Lt. Hembro H.Q. Scaling returned from Brasling Course 4/8/16. Comenced at "D" Coy from 5/8/16. | |
| | 7.8.16 | | 2nd Lt. H.G. Fulham to command "A" Coy from 7/8/16. | |
| | 8.8.16 | | 2nd Lt. E.A. Matthews appointed "Signalling" Intelligence & Sniping Officer 8/8/16. | |
| | 6.8.16 | | The Battalion came out of front line being relieved by 4th Battalion Middlesex Regt. and took over Support Line in CABARET ROUGE — ALHAMBRA and COLISEUM. | |
| | 9/8/16 | | 2nd Lt. G.A. Hann rejoined Battalion from 63rd Brigade H.Qrs. the establishment having been reduced — Intelligence Officer not allowed. | |
| | 31.8.16 | | 2nd Lt. E.G.M. Crocker joined Battalion from Base 3/8/16. | |
| | 1/8/16 | | 2nd Lt. E.T. Morgan sick to Hospital 1/8/16. | |
| | 4/8/16 | | 2nd Lt. T.F. Wallis " " Hospital 4/8/16. | |
| | 9/8/16 | | 2nd Lt. A. Attoll sick to Hospital 9/8/16. | |
| | 13.8.16 | | The Battalion holding Support Line CABARET ROUGE — ALHAMBRA — COLISEUM was relieved by the 1/9th Bn Seaforth Regt on night of 12th–13th. 9th Division taking over the Line. The Battalion moved out by Coys. aerie independently to Fields in GOUY SERVINS. Resting during the morning and afternoon of 13th inst. Separated for COMTE ROUTE :— BOYAN — VILLERS au BOIS. Paraded in Plateau Square 6-45 p.m. 13/8/16. | |
| | 28/7/16 | | Major R.H. Huntington invalided to England on 28/7/16. struck off strength of Unit. | |

Maitland Hardyman 2nd Lt. Adjt.
8(5)/Bn Somerset L.I.

# WAR DIARY or INTELLIGENCE SUMMARY

Army Form C. 2118

| Place | Date | Hour | Summary of Events and Information | Remarks and references to Appendices |
|---|---|---|---|---|
| | | | Casualties | |
| | 11/8/16 | | 2nd Lt. H.P.K. Barker. Lewis Gun Course. | |
| | 12/8/16 | | 2nd Lt. V.G. Willatt. Sniping Course. | |
| | 13/8/16 | | 2nd Lt. A. Garrard. Physical Training Course. | |
| | 14/8/16 | | 2nd Lt. E.F.N. Crocker. Gas Course. | |
| | 21/8/16 | | A.J.P. Akerman. Trench Mortar Course. | |
| | 11/8/16 | | 2nd Lt. G.F. Foscher. Trench Mortar Course. | |
| | 12/8/16 | | 2nd Lt. T.C. Snow to 54th Genl Hospital 13/8/16. | |
| | 14/8/16 | | Capt. R.A.B.P. Watts joined Battalion 14/8/16 from Base. | |
| | 16/8/16 | | Major K.V.F. Campbell. President at Field General Court Martial, held at Hqrs. 8pm. Lincolnshire Regt. 10 a.m. 16/8/16. 2nd Lt. F.G. Holenn attached for instruction 16/8/16. | |
| | 14/8/16 | | Capt. R.A.B.P. Watts appointed 2nd in Command 14/8/16. | |
| | 14/8/16 | | Capt. H. Hussey to Command "A" Company 14/8/16. | |
| | 16/8/16 | | 2nd Lt. C.C. Fagan. Appointed Physical Training Instruction Officer. | |
| | 18/8/16 | | Capt. R.A.B.P. Watts. President Court of Enquiry on 40 francs public money of "C" Company. 18/9/16. 2nd Lt. L.O. Hayes & 2nd Lt. T.C. Snow were members. | |
| | 19/8/16 | | Capt. R.A.B.P. Watts was a member of Field General Court Martial held at Hqrs. 8pm Lincolnshire Regt. 10 a.m. 19/8/16. 2nd Lt. F.G. Holenn attached for instruction 19/8/16. | |
| | 18/8/16 | | 2nd Lt. A.H. Hoff to command "C" Coy vice 2nd Lt. F.G. Harlow 18/8/16. | |
| | 17/8/16 | | 5 Drinkers started C.B. Departed for Base 17/8/16. | |

Maitland Hardyman
2nd Lt. Act. Adj.
875/Pte. Seacoart. Lat.

# WAR DIARY
or
## INTELLIGENCE SUMMARY
(Erase heading not required.)

Army Form C. 2118

| Place | Date | Hour | Summary of Events and Information | Remarks and references to Appendices |
|---|---|---|---|---|
| | 13/8/16 | | 2nd Lt. F.G. Allum to command "Headquarters Coy" vice Lt. J.P. Wickman. | |
| | 14/8/16 | | Capt. A.W. Phillips struck off strength of unit being attached to 4th Army School of Instruction Zuytpeen 11/8/16. (date of departure 27/3/16) | |
| | 18/8/16 | | Draft arrived from 10.3 Infantry Base Depot (Somersets) 7 Sgts. 1 L/Sgt. 4 Cpls. 18/8/16 | |
| | 19/8/16 | | Draft arrived from 10.3 Infantry Base Depot (Somersets) 1 Sgt., 11 Privates. 19/8/16 | |
| | 21/8/16 | | Capt. R.A.D.P. Watts President. Court of Enquiry held at Paths "Here" on Enlist- Balance of 862-50 Francs, account of 2nd Coy. 12/8/16. 2nd Lt. P.R. Higson & 2nd Lt. P.T. Chafer in call were members 21/8/16. | |
| | 21/8/16 | | 2nd Lt. H.P.U. Bucket to be Battalion Lewis Gun Officer 21/8/16. | |
| | 22/8/16 | | Extract Seunten Gazette dated 18th 7/16 :- Somerset Light Infantry. — To be Temp. Captains. Temp. Lt. W.A. Thorne (June 7th). Temp. 2nd Lt. T.F. Wallis. (July 7th). Temp. 2nd Lt. A.H. Hall. To be Temp. Lieut. (June 7th). | |
| | 22/8/16 | | Working party of 254 O.R. & 11 Officers left Camp for work in line. Attached to 9th Div. for Platoons. | |
| | 23/8/16 | | The Remainder of Battalion & Transport left Camp 23/8/16 at 2 p.m. in route for Goey BERVINS, & took over billets previously occupied. | |
| | 16/8/16 | | 2nd Lt. J.R.D. Pol. sick to Hospital. 16/8/16. | |
| | 19/8/16 | | 2nd Lt. M.W. Maurice, sick to Hospital. 19/8/16. | |
| | 22/8/16 | | 2nd Lt. A.P. Morgan Returned from Hospital. 22/8/16. | |
| | 25/5/16 | | Capt. R.A.D.P. Watts President at Court of Enquiry to inquire into the illegal absence of No. 15534 Pte Williams W. "J" Coy. | |
| | 25/8/16 | | L/Cpl Paisale sent to Base arrest age. | |
| | 26/8/16 | | Capt. E.W. Clark Doyle was a member of a F.G.C.M. & 2nd Lt. F.G. Allum attended for 8751/Pte. Somerset L.I. | |

Michael Henderson
2nd Lt. A.S.P.Adj.
8751/Pte Somerset L.I.

# WAR DIARY
## or
## INTELLIGENCE SUMMARY
(Erase heading not required.)

Army Form C. 2118

| Place | Date | Hour | Summary of Events and Information | Remarks and references to Appendices |
|---|---|---|---|---|
| | 27/8/16 | | Instruction assembling at F.G.S. 8th Somerset Lt Inf. Infantry at 10 a.m. Sunday August 27th 1916. | |
| | 29/8/16 | | On a count of Inquiring held at Battalion H.Qrs on 25/8/16. No. 15.034. Pte Williams C. "A" Coy. 8/3 Bn Somerset Lt Infantry was declared a "Deserter". | |
| | 30/8/16 | | Lt. G.P. W. Kennan attached to 63rd Trench Mortar Battery. | |
| | 30/8/16 | | 2nd Lt. Bryant proceeded to attend Toward Warfare Course at Rouen. | |
| | " " | | 2nd Lt. H.G. Price to Hospital (sick). | |
| | " " | | 2nd Lt. L.S. Holmes " " (sick). | |
| | 30/8/16 | | 2nd Lt. P.C. Hynes. Appointed Assistant Adjutant. | |

Maitland Hardyman
2nd Lt. Act. Adj.
8(S) Bn Somerset L.I.

**Army Form C. 2118**

# WAR DIARY
## or
## INTELLIGENCE SUMMARY
(Erase heading not required)

Vol 13

8 Som LI

| Place | Date | Hour | Summary of Events and Information | Remarks and references to Appendices |
|---|---|---|---|---|
| SOUCHEZ, I | 2/9/16 | | The Battalion (exclusive of Working Party of 159 Other Ranks and 10 Officers notified by 9th Division) left Gouy SERVINS for HERMIN. Route:- ESTRÉE CAUCHIE - CAUCHIN LEGAL - HERMIN. Paraded in Chateau Square 12 noon. Capt. H. Bussey was Président and 2nd Lt. H.P.W. Barker 2nd L.P.P. Hayen were Members of a Court of Inquiry held at Butn. H.Qrs. at 9-30 am Sunday Sept 3rd 1916 to investigate & report upon a debit balance of 250 francs on the account of "A" Coy. | |
| | 3/9/16 | | Lt. Sentenced of 2 years imprisonment with hard labour passed upon 10/5749. Lt. J. Armstrong, has been remitted on the grounds that he was well reported on by his Commanding Officer since his sentence, and took his conduct in the battle of the Somme having been praised by his Commanding Officer. | |
| | 3/9/16 | | Capt. S. Bulcot rejoined the Battalion from Hospital 3/9/16. | |
| | 1/9/16 | | A draft of 6 O.Rs arrived from No 3 Infantry Base Depot 1/9/16. | |
| | 3/9/16 | | Capt. S. Bulcot took over Command of "D" Company from 3/9/16. Lieut F.G.A. Ham | |
| | 3/9/16 | | Capt R.K.B.P. Lluffs. attached 112th 113th from 3/9/16. | |
| | 6/9/16 | | 100 Other Ranks Belton Regt and 23 O.R. Hampshire Regt (attached to this Unit) went transferred as from 30/8/16, new numbers having been allotted. Lt. A.H. Huff was a member of and 2nd Lt. A.H. Hambyrden attended for instruction a Field General Court Martial assembled at Headquarters 10th York & Lancaster Regt at 10-30 am on Tuesday 6th Sept 1916 | |

S. Campbell
Major
Commanding 8th (S) Bn Somerset L.I.

# WAR DIARY or INTELLIGENCE SUMMARY

Army Form C. 2118

*(Erase heading not required.)*

Instructions regarding War Diaries and Intelligence Summaries are contained in F.S. Regs, Part II. and the Staff Manual respectively. Title Pages will be prepared in manuscript.

| Place | Date | Hour | Summary of Events and Information | Remarks and references to Appendices |
|---|---|---|---|---|
| | 10/9/16 | | The detail of Officers mentioned below will assemble at Battalion H.Qrs. Mess at 10-15 am tomorrow 11th Sept. 1916 to investigate & report upon the Kelvin balance, 302-50 hours the account of "B" Coy. President Capt S. Babot — Members 2nd Lt R.E. Harper, 2nd Lt T.C. Snead. | |
| | 13/9/16 | | 2nd Lt Fitzmaurice joined the Battalion from No 3 Infantry Base Depot. 13/9/16. | |
| | 11/9/16 | | 13 Privates joined the Battalion 11/9/16 from No 3 Infantry Base Depot. | |
| | 7/9/16 | | Lt. H.E. Burtenshaw temporarily employed with Royal Flying Corps 7/9/16 is struck off strength of Unit. 7/9/16. | |
| | 14/9/16 | | 2nd Lt H.G. Babot joined the Battalion from the Base on 14/9/16. | |
| | 15/9/16 | | Draft of 5 Privates arrived from No 3 Infantry Base Depot. 15/9/16. | |
| | 18/9/16 | | 1 Sgt and 2 Ptes went on Escort to England, left Rouen 17/9/16. (18/9/16 to 27/9/16 inclusive) | |
| | 21/9/16 | | 1 Pte went on Escort to England, left Rouen 21/9/16. (27/9/16 to 1/10/16 inclusive) | |
| | 11/9/16 | | 11 Other Ranks left Rouen, proceeded to Rest Camp Boulogne, for 14 days rest. | |
| | 27/9/16 | | 2 Lt A.H. Hull and 10 Other Ranks left Rouen, proceeded to Rest Camp Boulogne for 14 days rest. | |
| | 7/9/16 | | 2nd Lt F.G.M. Crockett was recommended as Instructor & proceeded to 37 Division Bombing School as Instructor & joined 7/9/16. | |
| | 13/9/16 | | 2nd Lt L.S. Holmes returned from Hospital. 13/9/16. | |
| | 13/9/16 | | 2nd Lt H.C.L. Barker sick to Field Ambulance 13/9/16. | |
| | 15/9/16 | | 2nd Lt F.H. Morgan returned from Hospital 15/9/16. | |

N. Campbell Major
Commanding 8 (S) Bn Somerset L.I.

# WAR DIARY or INTELLIGENCE SUMMARY

Army Form C. 2118

| Place | Date | Hour | Summary of Events and Information | Remarks and references to Appendices |
|---|---|---|---|---|
| | 27/9/16 | | Draft arrived 23/9/16. 1 Regtl. Qr Mr Sgt, 2 Corporals, 1 Lance Cpl. & 4 Privates from No. 3 Infantry Base Depot. | |
| | 9/9/16 | | 2nd Lt. G.A. Hicks, Physical Training Course at Berres 9/9/16. | |
| | 11/9/16 | | 2nd Lt. F.H. Baker, Gas Course at 37th Div. School 11/9/16. | |
| | 14/9/16 | | 2nd Lt. T.C. Snow, Lewis Gun Course 14/9/16. | |
| | 17/9/16 | | Capt. Col. G. Wright, Trench Warfare Course 17/9/16. | |
| | 16/9/16 | | 2nd Lt. H.G. Baker, Grenade Course, 37th Div. Bombing School. | |
| | 16/9/16 | | The Battalion left HERMIN for CAMBRAIN-L'ABBE, paraded at 9-30 am. Route :- GAUCHIN LEGAL - VESTREE - COUCHIE -. Took over huts & bivouacs in same. 1 Company in Billet. The former previously occupied by Stafford Regt. 9th Division. | |
| | 17/9/16 | | The Battalion left CAMBRAIN-L'ABBE for FOSSEUX, paraded at 7-30 am Route :- GRAND SERVINS, - COUPIGNY, skirting SAINS-EN-GOHELLE, went into billets at (Sheet 36.B S.E.) R.9.a.6.2. | |
| | 18/9/16 | | The Battalion took over line SOUCHEZ I. Right Batta. from DRAKE Bn. of Royal Naval Division. Company Commanders reconnoitred line in morning of 18/9/16. The Battalion moved in by parties at 6-45 pm. Signallers & Lewis Gun Sections at 1 pm. Via AIX NOULETTE. The Battalion on taking over Souchez I Right Bn.: the disposition is as follows :- "A" Company Souchez Post, "C" Gunton Road (Support Coy), "D" Company Right Sub Section, "B" Left Sub section, "H Bn", Headquarters Trench, Telmet Crater, 9 Company later. | |

W. Renshall Major
Commanding 8th (S) Bn Somerset L.I.

# WAR DIARY
## or
## INTELLIGENCE SUMMARY
(Erase heading not required.)

Army Form C. 2118.

| Place | Date | Hour | Summary of Events and Information | Remarks and references to Appendices |
|---|---|---|---|---|
| | 8/9/16 | | During the period the Battalion was holding the front line (Souchez I Right) Patrols went out nightly at various times to reconnoitre + to support before positions of the enemy. Information of importance was not forthcoming. The general situation throughout the period : Quiet. | |
| | 27/9/16 | 10-15 a.m. | The detail of Officers as mentioned below will assemble at Battn. Hqrs Mess at 10-15 a.m. Wednesday Sep 27 7/9/16 to investigate as to support from the debit Balance 8/5 francs the account of "B" Coy. President Capt. A. Hussey, Members 2n Lt. P.C. Hayne + 2nd Lt. I.C. Snow. | |
| | 23/9/16 | | 1 Sgt + 2 Privates were granted leave from 27/9/16 to 6/10/16 inclusive. Cpl. S. Butler Sick to Hospital 23/9/16 | |
| | 27/1/16 | | On the afternoon of 27th inst. 8 canisters fired from the German line & fell in "B" Coy area (Right subsector) 2 of which extremely ruined a Lewis Gun & its ammunition. No other flew in to 15 Bay very badly, no casualties, the gun was recovered later damaged some what + the ammunition collected. | |

M. Campbell Major
Comm. 8/7/79 Bn Somerset L.I.

# WAR DIARY
## or
## INTELLIGENCE SUMMARY.
(Erase heading not required.)

Army Form C. 2118.

| Place | Date | Hour | Summary of Events and Information | Remarks and references to Appendices |
|---|---|---|---|---|
| Souchez I | 30/9/16 | | The Battalion on 30/9/16 (then the Reserve Battalion, Souchez I, in Lorette Line, Battalion Headquarters being at Abbaye St. Nazaire) moved into the front line trenches (Souchez I Right) to relieve the 4th Bn Middlesex Regt. The Companies were stationed as follows. "A" Coy Right subsection, "C" Left subsection of Front Line, "B" Coy held Souchez Foss, "D" Coy in Bencere Rd (support line). Battalion enterprises were carried out each night, the endeavours were to locate enemy movements, ascertain how their line was held, seeking the opportunity of capturing a prisoner or prisoners, firing not of all points of information of interest. | |
| | 6/10/16 | | On the night of 6/10/16 the Battn was relieved by 4th Bn Middlesex Regt. The Companies moved to positions in Reserve (Lorette line) as of 30/9/16. During the stay of 6 days, the enemy artillery were very active with trench fires, on our front line, doing considerable damage to our defences & trenches. Occasional shells were directed on the Headquarters trench, one, and fell to hit, destroying a dug-out used by the Battalion Orderlies. | |

2353 Wt. W.2544/1454 700,000 5/15 D.D. & L. A.D.S.S./Forms/C. 2118.

# WAR DIARY or INTELLIGENCE SUMMARY

Army Form C. 2118.

| Place | Date | Hour | Summary of Events and Information | Remarks and references to Appendices |
|---|---|---|---|---|
| | | | No casualties were suffered. 1 Ptd was slightly wounded the first day of occupation (Coy) & one man was evacuated to C.C.S. with field shock. 41 Other ranks were detached from the Battalion on 30/9/16 to form a fig-out Coy, being out Billets in Aix Noulette, working under supervision of the R.E.s. | |
| Souchez II | 12/9/16 | | The Battalion relieved the 10th Bn. York & Lancaster Regt. in Souchez II on the evening of 12th inst. "E" Coy holding Central sub-section, "D" Coy left sub-section, "B" Coy the 1st Sub-section, "A" Coy, 2 platoons Morris trench, 2 platoons to Bajolle Line. During the stay in the line the situation was normal, the principal activity being enemy using trench pieces, trench mortars & minenwerfers, doing a good deal of damage to our trenches. Casualties sustained, 1 Coy Sgt Major & 1 Private killed, 2 Other Ranks shock, the former being buried in a dug-out which was blown in from the rear. Retaliations were called for with effect. | |

J.L.S.
Lt-Col.
Comm'd'g 8th (S) Bn. Somerset L.I.

# WAR DIARY or INTELLIGENCE SUMMARY

Army Form C. 2118.

| Place | Date | Hour | Summary of Events and Information | Remarks and references to Appendices |
|---|---|---|---|---|
| Souchez II | 16/9/16 | | The Battalion was relieved on the evening of 16/9/16 (SOUCHEZ II) by 31 Bn Canadian Inf. The unit moved by companies independently to VERDREL where the Battn was billeted until 18th proceeding on that date into Billets at: BETHONSART. On the morning of 20th inst the Battalion marched to ETREE-WAMIN halted for the night, moving again at 8.45 am on 21st to NIPPER where the Battn was accommodated in tents. | |
| 3/9/16 | | | On 22nd the Battn marched to RAINCHEVAL & went into billets. 4 Other Ranks proceeded on leave from 4/9/16 to 13/9/16 inclusive. | |
| 5/9/16 | | | 2nd Lt. W.R.B. Peel returned to the Battn from hospital 4/9/16 | |
| 29/9/16 | | | 2nd Lt. G.A. Hare to Command "D" Coy vice Capt S. Best to hospital 29/9/16. | |
| 7/9/16 | | | 2nd Lt. H.S. Bart to the "Signallers" vice 2nd Lt. A.E. Matthews. | |
| 9/9/16 | | | 4 Other Ranks proceeded on leave from 9/9/16 to 20/9/16 inclusive. | |
| 9/9/16 | | | Lt-Colonel W.J. Scott resumed command of the Battalion 9/9/16. | |
| 12/9/16 | | | 1 Pte proceeded to Base for England (Munitions Work) on 12/9/16. | |
| 24/9/16 | | | 2nd Lt. H.V. Clarke, invalided to England on 24/9/16. | |
| 11/9/16 | | | 2nd Lt. C.O. Tubbs joined the Battn 11/9/16. | |

J.W. Scott
Lt.Col.
Commanding 8/31 Bn. Inniskng. F.

2353 Wt. W.2544/1454 700,000 5/15 D.D.&L. A.D.S.S./Forms/C. 2118.

Army Form C. 2118.

# WAR DIARY
## or
## INTELLIGENCE SUMMARY.
*(Erase heading not required.)*

Instructions regarding War Diaries and Intelligence Summaries are contained in F. S. Regs., Part II. and the Staff Manual respectively. Title pages will be prepared in manuscript.

| Place | Date | Hour | Summary of Events and Information | Remarks and references to Appendices |
|---|---|---|---|---|
| | 12/10/16 | | Lieut. Fitzmaurice to Command "A" Coy. vice Capt. H Hussey. to England (13/10/16) | |
| | 13/10/16 | | 2nd Lt. W.B. Tubbs to be "Battalion Bombing Officer" vice 2nd Lt. F.G. Williams to "A" Coy. 13/10/16. | |
| | 13/10/16 | | 2nd Lt. O.D Tubbs to Lewis Gun Sect. MGy Company vice 2nd Lt. Fizattume. 13/10/16. | |
| | 13/10/16 | | Capt. H Hussey. proceeded to England on Leave 13/10/16 (struck off strength of Unit) | |
| | 14/10/16 | | Strength of 58 Other Ranks arrived from No 3 Infantry Base Depot 14/10/16. | |
| | 16/10/16 | | " 8 " " " " " 16/10/16. | |
| | 17/10/16 | | " 8 " " " " " 17/10/16. | |
| | 17/10/16 | | 1 O.R. proceeded on leave from 17/10/16 to 25/10/16 inclusive. | |
| | 24/5/16 | | 16 O/ Sgts. (7 F/Sgts, 18 Cpls) were confirmed in their rank (Butln Orders 660. 24/10/16) | |
| | | | Capt S Baker, invalided to England on | |
| | | | 2nd Lt. C.S. Holmes invalided to England on | |
| | 23/10/16 | | Strength of 10 Other Ranks from No. 3 Infantry Base Depot joined Unit, 23/10/16. | |
| | 17/10/16 | | Major M.D.H. Campbell, invalided to England 17/10/16 | |
| | 26/10/16 | | Strength of 5 Other Ranks from No. 2 I.B.D joined Unit on 26/10/16. | |
| | 27/10/16 | | 9 Privates were transferred to 65 Machine Gun Coy. as from 27/10/16 | |
| | 28/10/16 | | Strength of 3. O.Rs joined Unit from No 3 I.B.D. on 28/10/16. | |

[signatures]
Commanding 8th (S/M Reserve) S.L.I.

**Army Form C. 2118.**

# WAR DIARY
## or
## INTELLIGENCE SUMMARY.
*(Erase heading not required.)*

Instructions regarding War Diaries and Intelligence Summaries are contained in F. S. Regs., Part II and the Staff Manual respectively. Title pages will be prepared in manuscript.

| Place | Date | Hour | Summary of Events and Information | Remarks and references to Appendices |
|---|---|---|---|---|
| | 25/10/16 | | 2nd Lt W. Keller transferred to Royal Flying Corps. 25/10/16. | |
| | 25/10/16 | | 1 O.R. proceeded to England (furlough) on 25/10/16 | |
| | 26/10/16 | | 2nd Lt. E.A. Hines sent to Hospital 26/10/16. | |
| | 16/10/16 | | 2nd Lt. H.E. Matthews sick to Hospital 16/10/16 | |
| | 25/10/16 | | Capt. Cartwright returned from leave 25/10/16. | |
| | 27/10/16 | | Capt. Cartwright took over command of "B" Coy. from 2nd Lt. F.H. Eveleigh 27/10/16 | |
| | 26/10/16 | | 2nd Lt F.R. Mellor took over command of "B" Coy. from 2nd Lt. E.A. Hines 26/10/16 | |
| | 27/10/16 | | 2nd Lt. F.G. Hudson returned from leave | 27/10/16 |
| | 27/10/16 | | 2nd Lt. W.R. Baker " " " | 27/10/16 |
| | 27/10/16 | | 2nd Lt. E.N. Morgan " " " | 27/10/16 |
| | 30/10/16 | | 2nd Lt F.R. Mellor to hospital (sick) 30/10/16 | |
| | 30/10/16 | | L/Cpl to hospital (sick) 30/10/16 | |
| | 30/10/16 | | The Battalion left RAINCHEVAL for BEAUVAL at 1 p.m. on 30/10/16 + went into billets | |

Signed
Commanding 13th Bn Somerset L.I.

## "A" Form.
### MESSAGES AND SIGNALS.

Army Form C. 2121.

| Prefix | m. | Words | Charge | This message is on a/c of: | Recd. at | m. |
| Office of Origin and Service Instructions. | | Sent | | | Date | |
| | | At | m. | Service. | From | |
| | | To | | | | |
| | | By | | (Signature of "Franking Officer.") | By | |

TO { Somerset / Middlesex

| Sender's Number. | Day of Month | In reply to Number | |
|---|---|---|---|
| Mm 858 | 18 | | A A A |

19th DIV. hope to advance against GRANDCOURT at 8.10 A.M. II Corps H.ARTY will keep its fire on PUISIEUX TRENCH fr. R.86.73 to its junction with ARTILLERY ALLEY until ordered to lift off. II Corps H.ARTY is also firing on the trench. 37 DIV. will be prepared to capture PUISIEUX & RIVER TR. as far NORTH as MIRAUMONT ALLEY. 8" Somersets will attack PUISIEUX & RIVER TR. from R.86.73 to its junction with MIRAUMONT ALLEY. 4" MIDDX. will move by companies into ANCRE TR. as vacated by 8" Somersets & will be prepared to support Somerset attack on PUISIEUX & RIVER TR. PUISIEUX ROAD from R.80.00 to R.76.67 will be reconnoitred as a place of assembly by MIDDX. The attack will be ordered by the BDE. & the Somersets will be prepared to start at 11 A.M.

Achmuteca

| From | 63 I. Bde |
| Place | |
| Time | 8.15 A.M. |

The above may be forwarded as now corrected. (Z)

Censor. Signature of Addressor or person authorised to telegraph in his name.

*This line should be erased if not required.

| Place | Date | Hour | Summary of Events and Information | Remarks and references to Appendices |
|---|---|---|---|---|
| | 1/11/16. | | The Battalion remained at BEAUVAL until 12/11/16 training was thoroughly carried out (prior to operations in the line). | |
| | 12/11/16. | | The Battalion marched away from BEAUVAL for LEALVILLERS, via BEAUQUESNE - RAINCHEVAL - ARQUEVES and went into billets 12/11/16. | |
| | 12/11/16 | | While at LEALVILLERS the Battn. made final preparation for attack. | |
| | 14/11/16. | | The Battalion moved from LEALVILLERS about 10 a.m. to HEDUVILLE via ACHEUX - FORCEVILLE. The Battn. made a halt about 2 p.m. leaving again at 5-30 p.m. for ENGLEBELMER, assembling there, before going forward to take over the line, to continue the advance commenced on 11/11/16. <br><br>The Transport and reserve reinforcements were Brigaded at a point S.E. of ENGLEBELMER, (under canvas) | |

J W Scott
8th (S) Bn Somerset L.I. Lt. Col.

| Place | Date | Hour | Summary of Events and Information | Remarks and references to Appendices |
|---|---|---|---|---|
| | 24/11/16. | | On the morning of 24/11/16 the transport, cooks etc. moved to billets in ENGLEBELMER, to await the arrival of the Battalion on being relieved in the line. | |
| | 25/11/16. | | The Battalion marched from ENGLEBELMER to MAILLY MAILLET, took over billets for the night. | |
| | 26/11/16. | | Left Mailly Maillet for SARTON via BEAUSSART - BERTRANCOURT - BUS les ARTOIS - AUTHIE - THIEVRES, a distance of 10 miles covered in 4½ hours 5 men fell out, went into billet leaving again on 29/11/16 for RAINCHEVAL via MARIEUX. | |
| | 3/11/16. | | 2nd Lt W.R.B.Peel sick to Hospital 3/11/16. | |
| | 4/11/16. | | Draft of 9 Privates joined the Battn. 4/11/16. | |
| | 5/11/16. | | 2nd Lt A.P.Morgan sick to Hospital 5/11/16. | |
| | 4/11/16. | | Lt.H.Pike. returned from Hospital 4/11/16. | |
| | 6/11/16. | | 2 Other Ranks. proceeded on leave to England from 6/11/16 to 15/11/16 inclusive. | |
| | 6/11/16. | | 2nd Lt M.K.F.Saunders joined the Battalion from No. 3 Infantry Base Depot 6/11/16. | |
| | 6/11/16. | | 2nd Lt J.R.Mellor returned from Hospital 6/11/16. | |
| | 7/11/16 | | 2nd Lt P.F.M.Hooper joined the Battalion from No. 3 Infantry Base Depot. 7/11/16. | |
| | 8/11/16 | | 2nd Lt W.R.B.Peel returned from Hospital 8/11/16. | |
| | 8/11/16 | | 2nd Lt K.E.King-King. joined the Battalion from No. 3 Infantry Base Depot. 8/11/16. | |
| | 9/11/16 | | Draft of 1 Sgt, 1 Cpl, 1L/c, and 5 Ptes joined the Battalion from No. 3 I.B.D. 9/11/16. | |
| | 10/11/16 | | Major D.W.C.Davies Evans arrived 10/11/16 being attached. | |
| | 12/11/16 | | Lt H.Pike. and 1 Pte proceeded on leave to England from 12/11/16 to 21/11/16 inclusive. | |
| | 14/11/16 | | 2nd Lt R.L.Sargeant joined Unit 14/11/16 | |
| | do. | | 2nd Lt J.H.B.Gegg. joined the Battalion 14/11/16. | |

Lt Col.
8th (S) Bn. Somerset Light Infantry.

# WAR DIARY or INTELLIGENCE SUMMARY.

| Place | Date | Hour | Summary of Events and Information | Remarks and references to Appendices |
|---|---|---|---|---|
| | 17/11/16. | | 2nd Lt F.G.Hinton. sick to Hospital. 17/11/16. | |
| | 19/11/16 | | Capt A.H.Hall Killed in Action 19/11/16. | |
| | 16/11/16 | | Lt L.Fitzmaurice Killed in Action 16/11/16. | |
| | 19/11/16 | | Lt. F.H.T.Joscelyne Killed in Action. 19/11/16. | |
| | 16/11/16 | | 2nd Lt B.T.Chippindall Killed in Action. 16/11/16. | |
| | 19/11/16 | | 2nd Lt J.H.M.Hardyman. Wounded in Action. 19/11/16. | |
| | 14/11/16 | | 2nd Lt W.R.B.Peel. Wounded in Action 14/11/16. | |
| | 19/11/16 | | 2nd Lt F.H.Baker sick to Field Ambulance 19/11/16 returned to unit 26/11/16. | |
| | 19/11/16 | | 2nd Lt F.G.Adlam sick to Field Ambulance 19/11/16 returned to duty 27/11/16. | |
| | 19/11/16 | | 2nd Lt C.B.Tubbs sick to Hospital 19/11/16. | |
| | 19/11/16 | | 2nd Lt E.G.M.Crocker Wounded in Action. 19/11/16. | |
| | 14/11/16 | | 2nd Lt J.R.Mellor sick to hospital 14/11/16. | |
| | 19/11/16 | | 2nd Lt K.E.King-King. Wounded in Action 19/11/16. | |
| | 17/11/16 | | Draft of 5 Other Ranks (Signallers) joined unit 17/11/16 | |
| | 20/11/16 | | Draft of 1 C.S.M., 1 Sgt, 1Cpl, and 90 ptes joined the Battalion from the base 20/11/16. | |
| | 23/11/16 | | Draft of 5 Other Ranks joined Unit 23/11/16. | |
| | 23/11/16. | | 2nd Lt G.F.Gibbs joined unit from Base. 23/11/16. | |
| | 24/11/16 | | 2nd Lt A.H.Llewellyn joined Battalion. 24/11/16. | |
| | 24/11/16 | | Draft of 2 O.R. joined Unit 24/11/16. | |
| | 26/11/16 | | 3 Other Ranks proceeded on leave to England from 26/11/16 to 5/12/16. inclusive. | |
| | 27/11/16. | | 4 Other Ranks proceeded on leave to England from 27/11/16 tp 6/12/16 inclusive. | |
| | 19/11/16 | | 2nd Lt G.F.Gibbs to be Battalion Bombing Officer vice 2nd Lt C.B.Tubbs (sick) 19/11/16. | |
| | 19/11/16 | | 2nd Lt F.C.Hagon to Act Adj. from 19/11/16 vice 2nd Lt J.H.M.Hardyman (Wounded) | |
| | 28/11/16. | | 5 Other Ranks Draft arrived 28/11/16. | |
| | 28/11/16. | | No. 15656 Pte Forster A. "D"Coy. having been released on suspension of sentence (Authority A.G. G.H.Q. B/759 d/- 18/11/16 rejoined unit on 26/11/16. | |
| | 5/11/16. | | No. 15349 L/c Young F. was tried by F.G.C.M. on 3/11/16 on the following charges (1) neglect to the prejudice of good order and military discipline (A.A.40) Firing a live round during Lewis Gun Instruction and thereby wounding two men. | |

W Scott Lt.Col
8th (S) Bn. Somerset L.I.

| Place | Date | Hour | Summary of Events and Information | Remarks and references to Appendices |
|---|---|---|---|---|
| | | | (2) Conduct to the prejudice of good order and military discipline (A.A.40). being in possession of a live round during Lewis Gun Instruction contrary to orders. He was found guilty of both charges and sentenced to 3 months imprisonment with hard labour. The sentence was confirmed and commuted to 3 months F.P. No. 1. G.O.C. 4/11/16. | |
| | 6/11/16 | | (London Gazette) Temp. 2nd Lt F.H.T.Joscelyne to be Temp. Lieut. ( July 22nd 1916.) | |
| | 11/11/16 | | The sentence of 15439 Pte Young, viz 3 months F.P. No. 1. has been commuted to 3 months F.P. No. 2. by G.O.C. 37th Div. 11/11/16. | |
| | 28/11/16 | | 2 Sgts left the Battn for Cadet School "Blendecques" for training. | |
| | 29/11/16 | | 2nd Lt F.H.Baker proceeded on leave to England from 30/11/16 to 10/12/16 inclusive. | |

Lt. Col.
8th (S) Bn. Somerset Light Infantry.

14/15.11.16. Midnight.
Moved into support under shelter of a high bank near
STATION ROAD West of BEAUCOURT and dug in.
16/11/16 Improved shelter - searched German Dug-outs which
were full of material and sent back amongst other articles
3 German made Stokes Mortars.
Whole battalion employed in carrying parties for 10 York &
Lancs and digging in ENGINE TRENCH.
Shelled intermittently but few casualties.
17/11/16 "C"Company moved out east of BEAUCOURT and took up a
position holding ANCRE TRENCH and BOIS d' HOLLANDE
facing PUSIEUX TRENCH. In the early morning drove in
hostile bombing party. Remainder employed in carrying parties.
Shelled intermittently most of the afternoon and had
15 casualties in one carrying party.
9 p.m. Received Orders for operations on the 18th.
18/11/16.
Battalion moved off by companies starting at 1 a.m. through
BEAUCOURT and completed line of posts from
BOIS d' HOLLANDE in a Westerly direction across the open to
the PUSIEUX ROAD.
"C"Company on right, ANCRE TRENCH to BOIS d' HOLLANDE.
"B"Company, centre.
"C"Company, left.
"D"Company about ANCRE TRENCH with orders to reconnoitre
PUSIEUX TRENCH and establish strong points in that trench and
in PUSIEUX RIVER TRENCH if possible.
2 Stokes Mortars and 2 M/Guns were attached and were placed
to assist in the attack on PUSIEUX TRENCH.
Snow was falling all night and the patrols on advancing
encountered hostile patrols out in front of PUSIEUX TRENCH
in shell holes and were unable to get near the trench.
6-10 a.m. Attack by 2nd Corps South of ANCRE RIVER
started.
A Scotch mist obscured the view but the advancing troops
could be seen.
9-20 a.m. Received orders to be prepared to attack
PUSIEUX and PUSIEUX RIVER TRENCH from S. end to its
junction with MIRAUMONT ALLEY supported by
4th Bn. Middlesex Regt.

Lt.Col.
8th (S) Bn. Somerset Light Infantry.

2nd Corps were attacking GRANDCOURT at 8 a.m.
The order to move was to be sent later.
Sent out preparatory orders for attack but time was
insufficient for receipt of the order owing to difficulty of
crossing very heavy ground under fire before 10-40 a.m.
when the order to attack at 11 a.m. was received.
The intermediate order containing details of barrage fire and
the order to move was not received till 11-25 a.m.
10-40 saw O.C. "C" and "D"Coys and ordered attack to be made
by "D"Coy. and half "C"Coy. on PUSIEUX TRENCH South of
MIRAUMONT ROAD as the most favourable ground,
remainder of "C"Coy. North of the road to cooperate.
11 a.m. 4th Middlesex began to arrive.
Attack commenced under heavy rifle fire from PUSIEUX TRENCH
and the river banks which caused most of our casualties :
shelling all day was very slight.
11-20 a.m. C.O. went forward to reconnoitre - found that the
attacking companies who had been advancing from shell hole
to shell hole were were under quite a heavy fire from
our own guns:
Stopped the attack went back and stopped our own guns.
Consulted with O.C. Middlesex with a view to fresh attack
under new barrage later, and gave orders for patrols to push
on if possible.
12 noon (about.) Bombing patrols entered trench and captured 20 Germans
in dug-out: "D"Company followed and consolidated the trench
south of the road.
Bombs ran short at one time but others were soon got up.
One Company Middlesex was sent up to support and later a
second Company: at the same time covering barrage was asked for
on PUSIEUX TRENCH north of the road. Meanwhile "A" and
"B" Companies had withdrawn from the line occupied in
accordance with the orders to attack. Casualties wery heavy.
4 Officers were killed including 3 Company Commanders and up
to 100 Other Ranks were casualties.
1 p.m.(about) 'Could see that attack on GRANDCOURT had
failed: about 100 men were visible coming back or moving
along railway line, S of ANCRE TRENCH.
PUSIEUX TRENCH was held but no further advance was made.

Lt. Col.
8th (S) 'Bn. Somerset Light Infantry.

| Place | Date | Hour | Summary of Events and Information | Remarks and references to Appendices |
|---|---|---|---|---|
| | | | 2-30 p.m. Sent the Bombing Officer 2nd Lt C.B.Tubbs to take Command of "A"Coy. and explain situation to "B"Coy. who were still under very heavy sniping fire.<br>3-30 p.m. Gave 2nd Lt C.B.Tubbs orders to re-occupy the line of posts as held in the early morning which was done at dusk.<br>7 p.m. onwards - 4th Middlesex took over PUSIEUX and ANCRE TRENCHES entirely and the line of posts was relieved by 2 Companies 10th York and Lancs.<br>Battalion withdrew into support in trenches and quarry just East of BEAUCOURT by about 10 p.m.<br>4 Officers had been wounded including the Adjutant 2nd Lt J.H.M.Hardyman who had gone round Companies to explain the situation in the afternoon.<br>2nd Lt F.H.Baker acted as Adjutant.<br>19/11/16 Remained in support.<br>At night parties went out and brought in the 4 Officers who were killed. They were buried near STATION ROAD.<br>Intermittent shelling all day.<br>The Officers left behind came up and 2nd Lt P.C.Hagon took over the duties of Adjutant.<br>20/11/16 Intermittent shelling all day.<br>XXXXXXXX Relieved by 1 Coy. 7th South Staffords and moved at dusk into old German 2nd Line.<br>21/11/16 Cleaning up and carrying parties at work.<br>22/11/16 Parties clearing the battle field at work. and Dug-out platoon sent up to Beaucourt trench.<br>23/11/16 3-30 to 9-30 p.m. Stood to in reserve to 111th Bde.<br>24/11/16 9 a.m. Left trenches and marched to ENGLEBELMER.<br><br><br><br>Lt. Col.<br>8th (S) Bn. Somerset Light Infantry. | |

| 1/12/16. | The Battalion left RAINCHEVAL for BEAUQUESNE 1/12/16 and went into billets. |
|---|---|
| | While at BEAUQUESNE the battalion carried out training daily. |
| 14/12/16 | Left BEAUQUESNE 14/12/16 for OCCOCHES? "B""C""D" went into billets there, "A"Coy. being billeted at OUTREBOIS& - Route taken, TERRAMESNIL - DOULLENS. |
| 15/12/16. | The Battalion left OCCOCHES about 11-15 a.m. proceeded to march to LIGNY, via NEUVILLETTE - BOUQUEMAISON - FREVANT - to LIGNY sur CANCHE. |
| 16/12/16. | Left LIGNY for VALHUON, via NUNCQ - HERLIN le sec - St POI. |
| 17/12/16. | The Battalion left VALHUON for BURBURE, via PERNES - FLORINGHEM - RAIMBERT. |
| 18/12/16. | Left again on the morning of 18/12/16 for L'ECLEME via LILLERS AND TOOK OVER BILLETS THERE & |
| | While in billets training was carried out and specialists were instructed and lectured. Cross country running took place, 2½ miles, 23 minutes allowed. |
| 22/12/16 | The Unit left E'ECLEME for the Brigade Area East of PARADIS and went into billets. |
| 9/12/16 | The Divisional Commander Inspected the 63rd Bde on 9/12/16, the following are his remarks passed. Considering the short notice, the Divisional Commander considers that the turn out was most creditable. |
| | The best turn out was undoubtedly that of the 8th (S) Bn. Somerset L.I. The Transport of this Battalion was By far the best turned out. |
| 1/12/16. | Major D.W.C.Davies Evans (Attached to the Battalion) having now been posted is taken on the strength. (Authority A/845 from A.G. d/- 28/11/16.) |
| 1/12/16 | Draft of 1 L/c, & 5 Ptes (Signallers) joined unit. |
| 2/12/16 | 1 Sgt, 1 Cpl, 3 L/c's, & 4 Ptes were granted leave to England from 3/12/16 to 12/12/16 inclusive. |
| 2/12/16. | The sentence of 12080 Pte Hamlin R. - 5 years P.S. commuted to 2 years imprisonment with H.L. suspended by G.O.C. 1st Army 23/11/16 was remitted by G.O.C. 61st Bde on 22/5/16 for good conduct. |

J.W.Scott
Lt Col.
8th (S) Bn. Somerset Light Infantry.

| Place | Date | Hour | Summary of Events and Information | Remarks and references to Appendices |
|---|---|---|---|---|
| | 4/12/16. | | Draft of 21 Other Ranks joined the Battalion from No. 3 I.B.D. on 4/12/16. | |
| | 4/12/16 | | 2nd Lt F.G.Adlam was granted leave from 5/12/16 to 15/12/16 inclusive. | |
| | 5/12/16. | | 2nd Lt A.P.Morgan having been invalided to England (Sick) on 14/11/16 is struck off the strength. | |
| | 5/12/16. | | Major D.W.C.Davies Evans was appointed President of and 2nd Lt T.C.Snow attended for instruction a Field General Court Martial assembling at the Headquarters of 63rd Trench Mortar Battery at TERRAMESNIL at 10 a.m. on 9/12/16. | |
| | 6/12/16 | | 9 Other Ranks were granted leave from 7/12/16 to 16/12/16 inclusive. | |
| | 10/12/16 | | Draft of 53 Other Ranks joined the Battalion from No. 3 I.B.D. 10/12/16. | |
| | 10/12/16 | | Draft of 10 Other Ranks joined the Battalion from No. 3 I.B.D. 10/12/16. | |
| | 9/12/16 | | 2nd Lt G.A.Ham to Command "C"Coy. vice 2nd Lt P.S.Bryant. | |
| | 11/12/16. | | 16224 Reg.Sgt.Major. Campbell D. was granted leave from 11/12/16 to 20/12/16 inclusive. | |
| | 11/12/16 | | Draft of 108 Other Ranks joined the Battalion from No. 3 I.B.D. on 11/12/16. | |
| | 13/2/16 | | 8 Other Ranks were granted leave to Eng. from 13/12/16 to 23/12/16 inclusive. | |
| | 13/12/16 | | Draft of 15 Other Ranks joined the Battalion on 13/12/16. | |
| | 21/12/16 | | Lt & Qr.Mr. J.J.Schooling and one Pte were granted leave to Eng. from 21/12/16 to 30/12/16 inclusive. | |
| | 22/12/16 | | Draft of 5 Other Ranks joined Battalion 22/12/16. | |
| | 22/12/16. | | 2nd Lt R.W.Heal joined the Unit 22/12/16. | |
| | do. | | 2nd Lt E.T.Rowland joined the Battn. 22/12/16. | |
| | 23/12/16. | | 2nd Lt R.W.Bullivant joined the Battalion 23/12/16. | |
| | 23/12/16 | | 2nd Lt F.H.Baker to Command "C"Coy. vice 2nd Lt G.A.Ham from 23/12/16. | |
| | 23/12/16. | | 7 Other Ranks were granted leave to Eng. from 23/12/16 to 2/1/17 inclusive. | |

Lt Col.
8th (S) Bn. Somerset Light Infantry.

| | Place | Date | Hour | |
|---|---|---|---|---|

24/12/16  2nd Lt T.C.Snow has been detailed to attend for
 instruction a Field General Court Martial
 assembling at the Headquarters of 4th Middlesex
 Regt. at 10-30 a.m. on Thursday 28th Dec 1916.
25/12/16 2nd Lt F.J.Clark joined the Battalion 25/12/16.
 do.   2nd Lt F.R.Cocksley    do.   do.   25/12/16.
 do.   2nd Lt T.C.Snow to be assistant Adjutant 25/12/16.
 do.   2nd Lt G.F.Gibbs to be O.C."H.Q" Coy. vice 2nd Lt
        T.C.Snow. 25/12/16.
26/12/16 1 Sgt proceeded to Eng. on 18/12/16 to take Temp.
         Commission.
26/12/16 6 Other Ranks were attached to the Machine Gun Corps
         (Heavy Branch) 26/12/16.
27/1/16. No. 30020 Pte Eastell F. (Att. 63rd T.M.B.)
         was tried by F.G.C.M. on 9/12/16 for
         "Neglect to the prejudice of good order and Military
         Discipline" (Self inflicted wound.)
         he was found guilty and sentenced to 1 month
         F.P. No. 1., the above sentence has been confirmed and commuted
         to 1 month F.P. No. 2.
27/12/16. The following N C O's and man have been awarded the
          MILITARY MEDAL&
          15760 L/c Ballantyne T.
          10001 L/c Crockford J.
          15734 Cpl Waters J.
          30041 Pte Hill M.
          13442 Cpl Sibley T.
           6434 Sgt Taylor J.
28/12/16 2nd Lt P.C.Hagon and 9 Other Ranks were granted
         leave to Eng. from 29/12/16 to 8/1/17 inclusive.
         2 Other Ranks were granted leave from 29/1/16 to
         29/1/17 inclusive (one month)
28/12/16. 2 Other Ranks joined the Battalion from No. 3 I.B.D.
          28/12/16.
18/12/16 2nd Lt J.H.B.Gegg went on General Course.
28/12/16 2nd Lt R.W.Heal went on course 28/12/16.
27/12/16 2nd Lt A.Garrad went on Lewis Gun Course.
30/12/16 2nd Lt E.T.Rowland went on sniping Course.
 9/12/16 2nd Lt G.A.Ham. returned from Hospital.
22/12/16 2nd Lt G.A.Ham went to Field Ambulance.
30/12/16 1 Sgt proceeded to England to take Temp. Commission.

                                  Jw Scott
                                           Lt Col.
                  8th (S) Bn. Somerset Light Infantry.

| Place | Date | Hour | Summary of Events and Information | Remarks and references to Appendices |
|---|---|---|---|---|
| | 30/12/16 | | 7 Other Ranks having been marked P.B. by the A.D.M.S. 37th Div proceeded to the Base. | |
| | 30/12/16 | | The Divisional Commander has much pleasure in recording that the Corps Commander has on more than one occasion exprrssed his satisfaction at the smartness of the Divisional Guard when turned out to him and has particularly noticed guards of the 8 th Somerset L.I. | |

J.W. Scott
Lt.Col.
8th (S) Bn. Somerset Light Infantry.

162

Vol 17

WAR DIARY

8th Somerset

January 1917

| Place | Date | Hour | Summary of Events and Information |
|---|---|---|---|
| | 2/1/17 | | The Battalion left PARADIS for CROIX BARBEE and went into close billets, being support Battalion to 4th Middlesex in right subsection NEUVE CHAPELLE., While in billets the unit found working parties and training was carried out. |
| | 8/1/17. | | On 8/1/17 the Battalion took over the line relieving the 4th Middlesex Regt (Neuve Chapelle Right) while in the line wireing was carried out extensively with the assistance of working parties found by the 4th Middlesex, Patrolling was carried out with success on the night of 13/1/17. The remarks thereon by Brigade Commander are as Follows :- The Brigade Commander desired to express his great satisfaction at the very good work of and the valuable information obtained by the two parties which patrolled the enemy's wire on the night of 13/1/17. |
| | 15/1/17 | | The Battalion was relieved by 10 R.F's on 15/1/17 and proceeded to PARADIS and took over billets previously occupied. |
| | 27/1/17. | | Left PARADIS for Le TOURET, via VIEILLE CHAPELLE - LACOUTURE - and remained there, prior going into trenches (Right Subsection FERME du BOIS), part of the battalion in billet and remainder in huts. |
| | 28/1/17 | | On the morning of 28th inst the Unit made its way to the line (FERME du BOIS) subsection Right relieving 8th Battn. East Lancashire Regt. |
| | 25/1/17 | | The following are the remarks passed by Divisional Commander regarding the Inspection of 25th 8th (S) Bn. Somerset L.I. The turn out, discipline on parade and appearance generally of this battalion was very good, and reflects credit on the Commanding Officer. |
| | 3/1/17 | | 2nd Lt E.H.Morgan and 11 Other Ranks were granted leave from 3/1/17 to 13/1/17 inclusive. |
| | 3/1/17 | | 2nd Lt C.H.Thornton, & 2nd Lt H.C.Frost joined the Battalion from the Base on 3/1/17. |

| | Place | Date | Hour | Summary of Events and Information | Remarks and references to Appendices |
|---|---|---|---|---|---|

| | | |
|---|---|---|
| | 3/1/17 | The undermentioned Temp. 2nd Lts. to be Temp. Lts. |
| | | C.B.Tubbs.  1/9/16 |
| | | A.P.Morgan.  10/9/16. |
| | 4/1/17. | 10 Other Ranks joined the Battalion from No. 3 I.B.D. on 4/1/17. |
| | 6/1/17. | Lt.Col.J.W.Scott D.S.O. was granted leave to Eng. from 6/1/17 to 16/1/17 inclusive. |
| | 7/1/17 | 11 Other Ranks were granted leave from 8/1/17 to 18/1/17 inclusive. |
| | 9/1/17 | Capt H.Hussey joined the Battalion 9/1/17. |
| | do. | 2nd Lt G.A.Ham. invalided to England. |
| | do. | 2nd Lt F.G.Adlam attached to 63rd Bde for duty from 9/1/17. |
| | 11/1/17 | 1 Other Rank granted leave. 11/1/17 to 21/1/17 inclusive. |
| | 11/1/17 | 21 Other Ranks Joined the Battalion from No. 3 I.B.D 21/1/17. |
| | 12/1/17 | 1 Warrant Officer proceeded to England to Take Temp. Commission 12/1/17. |
| | 13/1/17 | Capt C.W.G.Wright and 11 Other Ranks were granted leave to eng. from 13/1/17 to 23/1/17 inclusive. |
| | 13/1/17 | 1 Sgt proceeded to Eng. to take Temp. Commission 13/1/17. |
| | 13/1/17 | 4 Other Ranks joined the Battalion from the Base 13/1/17. |
| | 15/1/17 | Capt P.Rowland, 2nd Lt C.A.Baird and 2nd Lt S.Goodman joined he battalion from the Base 15/1/17. |
| | 16/1/17 | 28 Other Ranks joined the Unit from Base 16/1/17. |
| | 16/1/17 | Capt H.Hussey to be Acting 2nd in Command from 9/1/17. |
| | 16/1/17 | 2nd Lt T.C.Snow. was granted leave from 16/1/16 to 26/1/17 inclusive. |
| | 18/1/17 | 2nd Lt V.G.Willatt and 11 Other Ranks were granted leave from 28/1/17 to 28/1/17 inclusive. |
| | 19/1/17 | 1 N C O proceeded to England to take Temp. Commission 19/1/17. |

*J.W.Scott*
Lt Col.
Commanding 8th (S) Bn. Somerset L.I.

| Place | Date | Hour | Summary of Events and Information | Remarks |
|---|---|---|---|---|

| | 19/1/17 | | 2nd Lt H.M.Boucher joined the Battalion 19/1/17. | |
| | 20/1/17. | | 2nd Lt C.C.Gordon joined the Battalion 20/1/17. | |
| | 21/1/17 | | Capt M.K.F.Sannders was granted leave from 21/1/17 to 31/1/17 inclusive. | |
| | 23/1/17 | | 12 Other Ranks ~~xxxxxxxxxxxxxxxxxxxxxxxxxx~~ were granted leave from 23/1/17 to 2/2/17 inclusive. | |
| | 24/1/17 | | Capt H.Hussey was detailed a member of a Field General Court martial assembling at the Headquarters 9th North Staffordshire Regt at 10 a.m. on Jan 24th 1917. | |
| | 29/1/17 | | 10 Other Ranks joined the Battalion 29/1/17. | |
| | 24/1/17 | | The following Officers and Other Ranks were granted decorations as under:- | |

MILITARY CROSS.

    2nd Lt FRANCIS BAKER.

    On the ANCRE in November 1916 this officer led the front of the attack on PUISIEUX trench with great skill and gallantry. He led a Company of men skilfully across shell holes under heavy fire, and materially assisted in capturing and consolidating the trench. His example and coolness were invaluable.

    2nd Lt CECIL HENRY TUBBS.

    On the ANCRE in November 1916. After being sent from Battalion Headquarters to take command of a company in the open whose officers were killed, performed most gallant conduct and skill in crossing the open under heavy fire many times, going from platoon to platoon explaining the situation.

His coolness and complete disregard of danger had a splendid influence on all.

DISTINGUISHED CONDUCT MEDAL.

    No. 9004 C.S.M. WILLIAM HENMAN.

    For conspicuous skill and gallantry on the 18th November and in particular for taking command of a large part of his company when no officers were present, his Company Commander being killed. He kept them together and assisted them greatly by his example and Coolness.

                                                       Lt Col.

            Commanding 8th (S) Bn. Somerset L.I.

DISTINGUISHED CONDUCT MEDAL.
-----------------------------

    No. 15674 Sgt WILLIAM HEDLEY.

    For conspicuous gallantry on the night of the 17th November when an enemy bombing patty attacked his post near PUISIEUX trench. He attacked the enemy single handed at once with bombs and drove them off. He performed excellant work throughout the operations.

| | |
|---|---|
| 12/1/17 | 2nd Lt A.E.Matthews to Hospital sick 12/1/17. |
| 26/1/17 | 2nd Lt A.E.Matthews returned from Hospital 26/1/17. |
| 10/1/17 | 1 Other Rank was wounded in action 10/1/17. |
| 14/1/17 | 1 Other Rank was wounded in action 14/1/17. |

                        *[signature]* Lt Col.
              Commanding 8th (S) Bn. Somerset L.I.

WAR DIARY
8th Somerset L.I.
Vol 18
Feb 1917

17 L

| Place | Date | Hour | Summary of Events and Information | Remarks and references to Appendices |
|---|---|---|---|---|

22/2/17
1 T.R. wounded, bullet.
23/2/17
1 O.R. wounded, T.M.

7/2/17.
2nd Lt F.G.Hinton and 5 other ranks granted leave from 8/2/17 to 18/2/17 inclusive.
Capt C.W.G.Wright was detailed a member of a F.G.C.M. held at H.Qrs 10 York and Lancaster Regt. at 10 a.m. 8/2/17.
2nd Lt C.H.Thornton attended for instruction.

11/2/17
14/2/17. 2nd Lt H.Ward joined the Battalion.
2nd Lt H.G.Baker was a member of F.G.C.M. assembled at H.Qrs 8th (S) Somerset L.I. 10 a.m. 17th 1917

16/2/17.
15674 Sgt W.Hedley has been awarded The MEDAILLE MXXXXXXXXX MILITAIRE for "gallantry and devotion to duty in action" date of award 7/2/17.
1 Other Rank proceeded to Eng. as candidate for Temp. Commission. 18/2/17.
1 Other Rank wounded in action (buried shell) 19/2/17.
London Gazette. The undermentioned Temp. 2nd Lts to be Temp. Lieutenants 19/11/16
  J.H.M.Hardyman.
  T.C.Snow.
  F.H.Baker.
The following Officers are confirmed in rank of 2nd Lts.
  2nd Lt S.Goodman.
  2nd Lt C.D.Baird.
1 Other Rank. wounded in action 22/2/17.
2 O.R. Accidentally wounded 23/2/17.

23/2/17.
Lt C.B.Tubbs. being pronounced P.B. is struck off strength.
2nd Lt L.H.Vaughan joined the Battalion. 23/2/17.

25/2/17.
Major D.W.C.Davie Evans granted leave from 26/2/17 to 7/3/17.
2nd Lt A.C.Baird proceeds to BETHUNE as Brigade Salvage Officer.
4 O.R. joined Battalion from No. 3 I.B.D. 6/2/17
1 Pte To Base under age 6/2/17.
Capt C.W.G.Wright to Field Ambulance (Sick) 8/2/17.
Major D.W.C.Davies Evans Returned from 8th Lincolns. 10/2/17.
1 Pte granted leave to Eng. from 13/2/17 to 23/2/17 inclusive.
Capt H.Hussey attached to 8th Lincolns 19/2/17.
Capt C W G Wright from Field Ambulance 21/2/17
2nd Lt T.C. Harris joined Battn. 27/2/17
2nd Lt A C J Gaudelet to F.A. 22/2/17

       Geo. Scott
       Lt Col.
Commanding 8th (S) Bn. Somerset Light Infantry.

(1)

**1/2/17**
The Battalion on being relieved in FERME de BOIS Sector
by 16th Royal Warwick Regt. (5th Div.) on Feb 1st 1917
moved out of the front line, enroute for BETHUNE.
The relief commenced at 10 a.m., platoons at intervals
proceeded to BETHUNE via Le TOURET - ESSARS.
On arrival (about 4 20 p.m.) was billeted at CASERNE
La FEUILLADE.
While billeted at BETHUNE the battalion carried out training
under the New French Organisation.

**13/2/17.**
The Battalion left BETHUNE on 13/2/17 for MAZINGARBE via
NOEUX les MINES. Took over Huts previously occupied by
8th Buffs.
Quartermaster's Stores being at Les BREBIS.

**19/2/17**
The Battalion moved into the line Fosse 14 BIS (LOOS) right Subsection
19/2/17 relieving the 4th Bn. Middlesex Regt.
"A" & "D" Coys. in support, "B" & "C" Front line.
"Battn. H.Qrs in Village (LOOS)

**25/2/17.**
ON night 25/26 Feb the Battalion was relieved by 4th Middlesex
Regt. The Battalion moved into the VILLAGE LINE
relieving the 10 York & Lancaster Regt., the relief not
being complete till early morn, owing to state of ground.

**3/2/17**
1 other rank proceeded to Eng. as candidate for Temp. Commission.
12 O.R. granted leave from 3/2/17 to 13/2/17 inclusive.
2nd Lt A.Garrad invalided to Eng. (Sick) 25/1/17.
1 Other Rank proceeded to Eng. as candidate for Temp.
Commission.
2nd Lt T.C.Snow. marked unfit by M.B. in Eng. is struck off
strength 3/2/17.
The following Officers having arrived from No. 3 I.B.D.
on 7/2/17 are taken on the strength.
    2nd Lt W.C.Whiting.
    2nd LT A.G.Swain.
    2nd Lt H.B.Smith.
    2nd Lt A.C.J.Gardner.

*J.W.Scott*
Lt.Col.
Commanding 8th (S) BN. Somerset Light Infantry.

**3/3/17.**
The Battalion was relieved in the trenches by the 14th Durham Light Infantry (Village Line, Loos) on the morning of the 3rd inst. They moved off at 200 yards interval between Companies and marched to billets in LABOURSE, Headquarters being in SAILLY.

**4/3/17.**
The Battalion moved off at 9 a.m.
Route: via BETHUNE - ANNEZIN -rriving in billets at LABEUVRIERES and LAPUGNOY about 3 p.m.
Headquarters being at LAPUGNOY.

**5/3/17.**
The Battalion moved off, route via, CHOCQUES - LILLERS - ST HILAIRE arriving in billets at RELY 4 p.m.

**9/3/17.**
The Battalion moved off at 9 a.m., Route: via NEDONCHELLE - FIEFS - TANGRY arriving in billets 3-45 p.m. at WESTRUS.

**10/3/17.**
The unit moved off via WAVRANS - HERNICOURT - ST POL - arriving in billets MONTS EN TERNOIS 1-30 p.m.

The remainder of the month has been spent in training, a number of officers have been attached for 2 days at a time to a Division in the line at ARRAS.

Lt Col.
Commanding 8th (S) Bn. Somerset Light Infantry.

# WAR DIARY or INTELLIGENCE SUMMARY

Army Form C. 2118.

| Place | Date | Hour | Detail Summary of. | Remarks and references to Appendices |
|---|---|---|---|---|

**1/3/17.**
1 Sgt proceeded to England as candidate for Temp. Commission.

**2/3/17.**
2nd Lt H.G.Baker granted leave from 2/3/17 to 12/3/17 inclusive
Capt P.Rowland proceeded to 37th I.B.D. as Reinforcement Instr.
2nd Lt V.G.Willatt to Field Ambulance 27/2/17.

**3/3/17.**
2nd Lt H.B.Smith to Divisional Bombing Course.
Lt F.H.Baker to be Acting Captain from 6/1/17.
2nd Lt R.W.Heal to Field Ambulance 3/3/17.

**4/3/17.**
2nd Lt H.O.Pring joined the Battalion 4/3/17.
Major E.T.Skae left the unit (having been attached for instructional purposes) on 5/3/17 and proceeded to join 72nd Bde 24th Div.

**7/3/17.**
2nd Lt R.W.Heal returned from Field Ambulance.

**11/3/17.**
1 L/c proceeded to Eng. as candidate for Temp. Commission.
Lt R.W.G.Husbands joined the battalion, and took over the duties of Acting Adjutant.

**13/3/17.**
2nd Lt H.G.Baker attached to 37th Divl. Signals.

**16/3/17.**
2nd Lt T1P.Harris to Divl. Bombing Course.
2nd Lt H.Ward to General Divisional Course.

**10/3/17.**
2nd Lt P.F.M.Hooper took over Command of "B"Coy. vice 2nd Lt H.M.Boucher.

**16/3/17.**
Lt J.H.M.Hardyman rejoined the Battalion and took Command of "B"Coy. vice 2nd Lt P.F.M.Hooper.

**18/3/17.**
1 L/c proceeded to Eng. as candidate for Temp Commission.

**25/3/17.**
2nd Lt P.C.Hagon proceeded to Calais to take over duties as Reinforcement Instructor from Capt. P.Rowland.
4 Other ranks to Base having been pronounced "P.B." by a Medical Board being unfit for further services at the front.
2nd Lt A.H.Llewellyn and 1 Sgt proceeded to Third XXX Army Infantry School Course.
2nd Lt R.L.Sargeant reported Accidentally Killed while attending 1st Army Infantry Course (25/3/17.)
Capt P.Rowland pronounced "P.B." on 21/3/17.

**27/3/17.**
2nd Lt P.F.M.Hooper granted leave from 27/3/17 to 5/4/17 incl.

**28/3/17.**
1 Sgt Proceeded to Eng. as candidate for Temp Commission.

**30/3/17.**
Capt S.Baker rejoined the Battalion.

J.W.Scott
Lt Col.
Commanding 8th (S) Bn. Somerset Light Infantry.

# WAR DIARY or INTELLIGENCE SUMMARY

8 Somerset L.I.

| Place | Date | Hour | Summary of Events and Information | Remarks and references to Appendices |
|---|---|---|---|---|
| | | | **APRIL WAR DIARY 1917.**<br><br>2nd Lt H.Ward to Field Ambulance. 30/3/17.<br>Captain S.Baker joined the Unit 30/3/17.<br>13/4/17.<br>15451 Pte Laverack G was awarded the "Military Medal" vide King's Birthday Honours Gazette.<br>23/4/17.<br>15360 L/c Cottrall A.E. proceeded to England as candidate for Temp. Commission.<br>27/4/17.<br>Major J.G.Underwood joined the Battalion from 6th S.L.I.<br>30/4/17.<br>Lieut.Colonel. H.K.Umfreville.D.S.O. joined the Battalion.<br>1/4/17.<br>Capt S.Baker to Command "B"Coy. vice Lt J.H.M.Hardyman.<br>3/4/17.<br>Capt M.K.F.Saunders was a member of a Field General Court Martial assembled at Headquarters at 4th Bn. Middlesex Regt at 10 a.m. 4/4/17.<br>2nd Lt C H Thornton attended for instruction.<br>4/4/17<br>The sentence of "Death" commuted to "3 years P.S. to be suspended " on 15537 Pte Williams has been remitted.<br>( G.O.C. 63rd Bde ) 31/3/17.<br>5/4/17.<br>Temp.Capt J.P.Akerman is struck off strength of Battalion<br>( A.G. G.H.Q. No. A /16119/170 d/- 28/3/17.)<br>( 37th Div. 302/47 A d/- 4/4/17.)<br>5/4/17.<br>2nd Lt A.C.J.Gardner having been evacuated to England is struck off strength. | |

H.K.Umfreville Lt Col.
8th (S) Bn. Somerset Light Infantry.

1/4/17.
The Battalion left Monts en Ternois on morning of
April 5th at 10 a.m.  enroute for LIGNEREUIL route
via AMBRINES  arriving in billets 11-30 a.m.

7/4/17.
The Battalion moved off 7-30 a.m. en route for
HAUTEVILLE arriving in billets at noon.

8/4/17.
The Battalion marched off to DUISANS at 7-55 a.m.
route via LATTRE-ST-QUENTIN arriving at billets
(huts) at 11/30 a.m.

9/4/17 to 12/4/17 inclusive Battalion in action.
(See operations)
Total Casualties. Officers 2. Other Ranks. 101.
"Wounded" 2nd Lt J.H.B.Gegg.
         2nd Lt H.C.Frost.
"Killed"  Other Ranks.      26.
"Wounded"   do.   do.       70.
"Missing"   do.   do.        5.
Battalion H.Qrs  situated in ARRAS.

12/4/17.
The Battalion came out of action night 12th billeted
one night in ARRAS.

13/4/17.
The Battalion marched to DUISANS and billeted (Huts)
for one night. Moving next morning to
AGNEZ les DUISANS. the battalion being in billets by
noon.

15/4/17.
The Battalion marched to BEAUFORT via
AVSNES les COMTE Arriving in billets 1-30 p.m.

19/4/17.
The battalion moved off 9-15 a.m. arriving in
billets MONTENESCOURT staying one night, from here the
battalion moved up to ARRAS and then into action
on 20th.

April 20th to 28th Battalion in action.
(See Operations)
Total. Casualties. Officers 18. Other Ranks. 296.
"Killed" Lt Col J.F.Scott D S O  23/4/17.
         2nd Lt L.H.Vaughan.      do.
         2nd Lt C C R Gordon.    28/4/17.
         2nd Lt G.F.Gibbs.        do.

                                    Lt Co.l
         8th (S) Bn. Somerset Light Infantry.

"Wounded" Officers.
    Capt C.W.C.Wright.    23/4/17.
    Capt S Baker.    do.  d. of w. 28/4/17
    Lt R.G.W.Husbands.    do.
    Lt F.G.Hinton.    do.
    2nd Lt F.J.Clark.    do.
    2nd Lt E.J.Rowland.    do.
    2nd Lt W.C.Whiting.    do.
    2nd Lt E.A.Matthews.    do.
    2nd Lt R.W.Bullivant.    do.  d. of w. 1/5/17
    2nd Lt P.F.M.Hooper.    do.
    Capt M.E.F.Saunders.    28/4/17.
    2nd Lt A.C.Owen.    do.
    2nd Lt R.W.Heal.    do.
    2nd Lt P.H.Morgan.    do.

"Killed" Other Ranks.    17.
"Wounded"  do. do.    180.
"Missing"  do. do.    99.

29/4/17.
Battalion relieved and moved back (motor lorries) to BEAUFORT.

                                          W.K.Umfreville Lt Col.
                        8th (S) Bn. Somerset Light Infantry.

| | | | |
|---|---|---|---|
| Place | Date | Hour | Summary of Events and Information |

## OPERATIONS 9th - 12th April.

9th April.
Moved about 2.30 p.m. from the assembly trenches to Battery Valley about H 27 a 06.
About sunset received verbal orders that 8th Som L.I. with 8th Lincolns on left would advance and occupy ORANGE HILL : and if 111th Bde were advancing push on and occupy LONE COPSE VALLEY.
Officers patrol sent off to locate the 111th Bde
Advancing to Brown Line about H 28 c S.E. which was held by H.L.I.
The right of this battalion a little to the South was in the air.
The officer's patrol (agreeing with the H.L.I.) reported 111th Bde on road in H 33 d.
2 Coys moved out to ORANGE HILL about H 35 a 05 with right thrown back and 1 Coy. in support about H 34 b 53.
A post was established about 300 yards South H.L.I. about H 34 central which came in touch with the enemy. This was relieved by 6th Camerons towards dawn.
About midnight I spoke to G O C on telephone and was instructed that Lincolns should push down to SUNKEN ROAD and send forward L platoon Som.L.I. towards head of LONE COPSE VALLEY.

April 10th.
In the early morning reports of enemy movements and digging in N of MONCHY reached me.
Also order that Brown Line would be attacked at noon followed later by attack of 111th Bde & 112th Bde on MONCHY, 63rd Bde in support on left.
About 10 a.m. sent 2 Coys. to make good LONE COPSE VALLEY and followed at once with rest of battalion when I saw my leading Company nearing the enclosures.

*[signature]* Lt Col.
8th (S) Bn. Somerset Light Infantry.

| Place | Date | Hour | Summary of Events and Information | Remarks and references to Appendices |
|---|---|---|---|---|
| | | | Noon. Position as follows. | |

Noon.
Position as follows.
   1 Coy. about H 36 c 3.4.
   1 Coy. about H 36 a 7.4.
   2 Coys. in valley.
   I then ordered 1 Coy. to advance to the crest and towards trenches in H 36 d N.E. if possible.
It came under very heavy fire and could not get on.
Meanwhile about 1 hour after I arrived.
8th Lincolns came up to support in H 36 a central.
Later:
   When the attack of 111th Bde was seen advancing 2 Coys attacked the enclosures on the North and got up to the hedges where they were stopped by machine gun fire: and the 111th were stopped on my right rear.
Position remained thus till 7-20 p.m.
10th April.
   Order received for advance at 7-30 p.m. on final objective by 8th Som.L.I. 8th Lincs, 4th Middlesex.
the 111th & 112th also to advance.
   My patrol to 13th R.F. returned about 8-45 p.m. to say the 13th R.F. had advanced and been cut up.
   Meanwhile I moved 8th Som.L.I. and 8th Lincs ready to advance on trenches in H 36 d but this did not mature.
9-30 p.m.
   Sent Coys back to their positions in line
H 36 c 54 - H 36 c 7.8.
   8th Lincolns on my left along bank in H 36 a
North of road.
Later:
Found 1 Coy. 4th Middlesex near Lone Copse
10 York and Lancs beyond them.

*(signature)* Lt Col.
8th (S) Bn. Somerset Light Infantry.

| Place | Date | Hour | Summary of Events and Information | Remarks and references to Appendices |
|---|---|---|---|---|
| | | | 11th April. 4-20 a.m. Received order that 15th Div. in conjunction with 111th Bde & 112 would attack east on original objective at 5-30 a.m. 6 a.m. about. 1 Battalion 15th Div advanced through me and captured trenches in H 36 d. 1 Battalion in support dug in on crest behind them. "Afternoon" Position remained there all day until order arrived that 63rd Bde would concentrate in H 35 d ready to support advance of 111th. No concentration was possible and when other 3 Battns. advanced to support 111th Bde 8th Som.L.I. remained in reserve in same position. 12th April 4 a.m. Moved back to H 33 d. | |

Lt. Col.
8th (S) Bn. Somerset Light Infantry

## OPERATIONS APRIL 22nd.

On 22/4/17 the 8th Bn. Somerset Light Infantry were resting in trenches (LAUREL CAM EFFIE) in France 51B N.W. X H.9.

LAUREL TRENCH was submitted to a heavy gas shell bombardment from 12-5 a.m. to 4 a.m. with desultory gas shelling until 6 a.m.

At 11-15 p.m. Companies moved forward independantly to the assembly trenches in H 11 c., and thence at 3 a.m.23/4/17 to in front of HYDERABAD WORK in H 12.a. and c.

At Zero hour the battalion was not in touch with the 8 Lincolns, as the 8th Lincolns were on the right of HYDERABAD WORK in H 11 c. in touch with the Black Watch of the 51st Division. For this reason in the first hour after Zero the 8th Lincolns was in support to the 8th Somerset L.I..

As the attack moved forward, the 8th Lincolns came up on the left of the 8th Somerset L.I. The 8th Somerset L.I. with the 4th Middlesex in front pressed straight on to the cross roads at I 7 a.5.3. During this period the Battalion H.Q. of the 8th Som.L.I. was in CLYDE TRENCH, with the Lincoln H.Q. just behind. Progress during the morning was slow, owing to direct rifle and machine gun fire. By noon the 8th Lincoln H.Q. had reached CUBA trench or its vicinity, having worked round by H 6.B. but a

party of our troops were still held up by a party of 50 or 60 Germans entrenched about H 12 b 8.2. These surrendered to the O.C. 8th Lincolns, who accompanied by 2 orderlies, approached them from the rear.

*signature* Lt Col.
8th (S) Bn. Somerset Light Infantry.

| Place | Date | Hour | Summary of Events and Information | Remarks and references to Appendices |
|---|---|---|---|---|
| | | | The 8th Somerset L.I. meanwhile had collected their main body in the sunken road south of the X roads in I 7 a. under the command of Captain Saunders and 2nd Lt Owen:- the only two Officers who remained in action until relieved. Lt Col J.W.Scott, his Adjutant, Headqrs, and the remainder of theof the Battalion were at about I 7 b.1. At this stage the Adjutant was wounded, and Lt Col. J.W.Scott. was killed, while the enemy in artillery formation came down over GREENLAND HILL to a trench about 800 yards of the sunken road running from the I 7 a 2.8. to I 7.c.7.8. - and parallel to it.

Captain M K F Saunders collected all Somersets and dug in CLASP TRENCH where he was relieved on the night 24/25.4.17. The 4th Middlesex were about 300 yards in front of the Somersets.
Capt Saunders established connection with the Lincolns on the left, and the troops (112th Bde) on his right.

Owing to the lie of the ground between the X roads at I 7 a 5.3. and I 2 c 3.5. the Somersets and Middlesex on the one hand and the Lincolns on the other believed that they had alone pressed forward with both flanks unsupported. This false impression was corrected at noon 23/4/17.

The afternoon of 23.4.17 was spent by the 8th Somersets in the consolidation of CLASP TRENCH. The relief was accomplished the same night without incident, the Battalion returning to HERON TRENCH about 200 strong in other ranks with Captain M.K.F.Saunders and 2nd Lt Owen.

J C Humfrieville Lt Col.
8th (S) Bn. Somerset Light Infantry | |

# WAR DIARY or INTELLIGENCE SUMMARY

*(Erase heading not required.)*

| Place | Date | Hour | Summary of Events and Information | Remarks and references to Appendices |
|---|---|---|---|---|

## OPERATIONS APRIL 28th 1917.

Reference Map 51 B. N.W.

The 8th (S) Bn. Somerset Light Infantry under Captain M.K.F.Saunders moved forward from HERON TRENCH XX (H 11 a.) and took up position in CUBA TRENCH I 7 a at 3 a.m. 28/4/17.

At Zero hour (4-25 a.m.) the Battalion followed the Barrage due east to CUTHBERT TRENCH where 2nd Lt F.R.Cooksley with 13 men was dropped to mop up and consolidate.

Then finding WHIP TRENCH ( I 2.c.) in front, the troops swung to the left to attack it. Finding no opposition, it was impossible to check their onward rush, which carried them in a North Easterly direction as far as RAILWAY COPSE.

Returning wounded reported that there was no opposition and they were confident that the village of FRESNES could have been easily taken had there been a few more troops.

Consolidation of WHIP TRENCH was at once proceeded with by the mixed collection of Somersets, Bedfords, etc., Many of those who swept on returned and joined the party in WHIP TRENCH.

The position was not modified by noon.

At about the 112th Bde left WHIP TRENCH and apparently vacated the areas "I" altogether.

This left 2nd Lt F.R.Cooksley with a party of 50 in CUTHBERT TRENCH in an isolated position.

At 11 a.m. 2 Coys of Middlesex made efforts to reach him but in my opinion, they, owing to the left, xxxx where they encountered machine gun fire, were unable to get forward.

*J.K.Umfreville* Lt Col.
8th (S) Bn. Somerset Light Infantry.

| Place | Date | Hour | Summary of Events and Information | Remarks and references to Appendices |
|---|---|---|---|---|
| | | | All R.E's, Pioneers, Stragglers, etc, were then withdrawn from CUBA CUTHBERT area, 2 Coys of N Staffs were ordered to hold the line of the road from the X roads asfar as possible, and 9th Division troops took over CUBA TRENCH. On the night 29/30.4.17. 2nd Lt F.R.Cooksley got in touch with the Seaforths in CUBA and was relieved.<br><br>J.K.Lempriere Lt Col.<br>8th (S) Bn. Somerset Light Infantry. | |

War Diary
8th Somerset L.I.
May 1917

Vol 21

| Place | Date | Hour | Summary of Events and Information | Remarks and references to Appendices |
|---|---|---|---|---|

## WAR DIARY
### MAY 1917.

**6.5.17.** 2nd Lt. T.P. Harris having been evacuated to England is struck off the strength (Auth. 3rd Army List No. 70.)
A draft of 92 Other Ranks arrived from No. 3 I.B.D.
Capt. R.A.B.P. Watts joined Battalion, and was attached to 10th Y & L. Struck off strength 7.5.17.

**7.5.17.** The following Officers joined Battalion :-
2nd Lt. H.R. KIRK
  "   C.D. HAGON.

**8.5.17.** A draft of 93 Other Ranks arrived.

**9.5.17.** Maj. C.M.A. Samuda joined Battalion and was attached to 13th Royal Fus. 10.5.17.

**10.5.17.** Draft of 73 Other Ranks arrived from No. 3 I.B.D.
Capt. F.H. Baker invalided to Eng.

**12.5.17.** One Other Rank joined from No. 3 I.B.D.

**14.5.17.** Draft of seven Other Ranks arrived from No. 3 I.B.D.

**16.5.17.** Draft of 12 Other Ranks     "     "     "
Maj. J.G. Underwood appointed President of F.G.C.M. assembled at H.Q. 8th Som. L.I.
2nd Lt. F.R. Cooksley took over command of "C" Coy vice 2nd Lt. F.S. Bryant.

**20.5.17.** 3 Other ranks granted leave from 20th to 30th inc.

**21.5.17.** 4 Other ranks granted leave 21st to 31st inc.

**22.5.17.** 9 Other Ranks     "     " 22nd to 1st inc.
2nd Lt. C.H. Thornton invalided to Eng. (Auth. 3rd Army List No. 72)

**24.5.17.** 5 Other ranks to Summer Rest Camp for 14 days.
9887 L/c Lyons F. to Boulogne for duty with Railway Construction Unit.

**25.5.17.** Three other ranks joined Battalion.

**26.5.17.** 2 Other Ranks granted leave from 26th to 5th inc.
2nd Lt. L.J.H. White joined Battalion from Base and posted to "B" Coy.
2nd Lt. H.J. Hunt joined Batt and took over command "A" 27.5.17.
2nd Lt. H.G. Baker rejoined Batt 27.5.17.

**27.5.17.** Took over command "D" Coy.

**28.5.17.** 2nd Lt. H.O. Pring rejoined Battalion from 37th Div. Depot.

6/6/17

J.K.Umfreville  Lt.Col.
Commdg 8th (S) Bn Somerset L.I.

# WAR DIARY or INTELLIGENCE SUMMARY

*(Erase heading not required.)*

| Place | Date | Hour | Summary of Events and Information | Remarks and references to Appendices |
|---|---|---|---|---|
| | | | **WAR DIARY.** **MAY 1917.** | |
| | 11.5.17. | | Extract from Brigade R.O. 544 dated 11.5.17 "The G.O.C. wishes to congratulate the following men to whom the Corps Commander has awarded Military Medals for acts of gallantry in the field near ARRAS April 9/13. 26537 Pte James A. 18792 Pte Dutch J. 15533 Pte Fryer A. 17477 Pte Hibbard B 14986 " Davis G.W. (Since "D" of "W") | |
| | 13.5.17. | | Battalion Sports were held. | |
| | 14.5.17. | | Copy of telegram received from Commander in Chief addressed to Third Army " I congratulate you and your troops on the complete success of the various attacks made yesterday and this morning. These successes are very satisfactory, not only in themselves but as showing that the enemy is beginning to weaken under the repeated heavy blows inflicted on him during all the hard fighting of the past five weeks" | |
| | 16.5.17. | | The Corps Commander has awarded the Military Medal to 16034 Pte Rowley W. for acts of gallantry in the field. (Authy 6th Corps R.O. 2121 of 12th May) The Military Medal Riband was this day presented by Brig. Genl E.L. Challinor D.S.O. Commdg 63rd Inf. Bde. to the following :- 26537 Pte James. A. 18792 Pte Dutch J. 15533 Pte Fryer A. | |
| | 17.5.17. | | Battalion left BEAUFORT morning of the 17th. arriving in Billets (Huts) SIMENCOURT route via Avesnes le Comte, Hauteville, WANQUENTIN, staying one night, leaving again 11 a.m. to DAINVILLE. Route via Beaumetz les Loges, Doullens Arras Road, arriving in billets 2 p.m. | |
| | 21.5.17. | | Battalion left BEAUFORT morning 21st at 10.30 a.m. and marched to ARRAS billeting in LEVIS BARRACKS. Extract from C.R.O. 2162 of 18.5.17. "The Army and Corps Commanders have been pleased to note that the Field Marshal Commanding in chief has under authority by his Majesty the King awarded the following decoration to the undermentioned:- 27644 Pte F. DOLLING D.C.M. 2/ | |

6/6/17                    Commdg 8th (S) Bn Somerset L.I.

# WAR DIARY
## MAY 1917.

**26.5.17.** The 17th Corps Commander has sent the following message to the Commander 37th Div. ( Maj. Gen. M. Bruce Williams C.B. D.S.O.) "I shall never forget your splendid Division for their grit and pluck. I wish very much we had you here with us again." It is hoped by the Div. Commdr that all ranks will hear this message.
He has confidence in the fact that they will do their best to maintain this great reputation earned in two Army Corps since the commencement of the battle of ARRAS.
The Corps Commander has awarded the Military Medals to the following N.C.O's and Men for Acts of Gallantry in the field (Authy C.R.O. 2200 dated 24.5.17)   9421 Sgt Butler S, 15203 Cpl Geach. 27582 Pte Worrell H. 7537 Pte Steele F.W.

**28.5.17.** Lt. H. Pike and 8 Other Ranks granted leave from 28th to 7th inc.
Battalion left Levis Barracks Arras afternoon 28th for the trenches, relieving 8th (S) Bn. East Lancs at a point North of the HARP Relief being complete by 7 p.m.
Held trenches until morning 31st when we were relieved by the 5th Gloucester Regt. relief being complete by Noon.

**31.5.17.** Battalion in billets Levis Barracks 31.5.17. The 17th Corps Commander has awarded the Mil. Med. to the following N.C.O's and Men for gallantry during the period "23rd to 30th April 1917." :-   7406 Pte Youdle W.   15419 Cpl Measures J.     15106 L/c Davis F.
16115 L/Sgt Henderson R.    11066 Sgt Franckom 14799  L/c Williams F.

[signature] Lt. Col.
Commdg 8th (S) Bn. Somerset Light Infy.

6.6.17.

War Diary

5th Somersets

JUNE 1917

SECRET

| Place | Date | Hour | |
|---|---|---|---|

## June
### War Diary 1917

| | | |
|---|---|---|
| | 1/6/17 | Bn left "LEVIS BARRACKS" afternoon of the 1st June embussing in the Rue de Lille, and arriving in billets at Manin 8p.m. |
| | 6/6/17 | Bn left Manin at 8a.m. en route for HERICOURT in busses, route via Beaufort, Liencourt, Frevant arriving in billets about noon. |
| | 7/6/17 | Bn moved off morning of the 7th en route for BERGUENEUSE route via Croisette, Pierremont, Monchy. |
| | 8/6/17 | Bn left Bergueneuse 8.30a.m morning of the 8th en route for FRUGES, route via Crepy, Verchin, arriving in billets 2p.m. |
| | 9/6/17 | Bn in training up to the 21st |
| | 22/6/17 | Bn left Fruges 7.30a.m. en route for LIGNY-LEZ-AIRE route via Beaumetz-les-aire, Laires, Febvin Pelfart, staying one day, moving again to STEENBECQUE morning of the 23rd at 4.45a.m. route via Rely, Lingham, Lambres and Aire. |
| | 24/6/17 | Left STEENBECQUE morning of the 24th at 5a.m. en route for ST SYLVESTRE CHAPPEL, route via Hazebrouck. |
| | 25/6/17 | Left St Sylvestre Chappel morning of the 25th at 5.45a.m. en route for SCHERPENBERG; route via Caistre, Fletre, and Meteren arriving in billets (huts) by noon. The Bde was inspected on the march by the 2nd Army Commander. |
| | 29/6/17 | Bn left Scherpenberg evening of the 29/30th and relieved 10th Bn York and Lancs in the Right Support Line. (L Section JOYE FARM to ROSE WOOD). |

　　　　　　　　　　　　　　　　　　　　　*[signature]* Lt Col.
　　　　　　　　　　　　　　　8th (S) Bn Somerset Light Infantry.

## June
## War Diary 1917.

2/6/17  The following Officers joined Bn this day
2nd Lt E.W.R.Blake, 2nd Lt W. Wood, 2nd Lt L.C.Bodey, 2nd Lt
A.J.Crease, 2nd Lt T.W.Adams. 10.R. granted leave from
2/6/17 to 11/6/17 inc. 20 O.R. joined Bn this day.
40.R. returned from rest camp.

4/6/17  16634 R.S.M. Campbell D.G. proceeded this day
to 8th East Lancs Regt. as temp. Qr.Mr. and Hon Lt
is struck off the strength. Auth. A.G. A/25742 D/4
1/6/17. 18926 Sgt Jennings R. proceeded this day to
Eng as Candidate for Temp Commission.

5/6/17  Lt A.H.Llewellyn and 7 O.R. granted leave from
5/6/17 to 15/6/17 inc. C.S.M.Rockey F. appointed Regt
Sgt Major vice D.G.Campbell.

9/6/17  10.R. granted leave from 9/6/17 to 19/6/17 inc
The following Officers joined Bn this day. 2ndLt G.Durston
2nd Lt H.de F. Ford, 2nd Lt R.P.Braund.

10/6/17  Major J.G.Underwood was appointed President of
a F.G.C.M. assembled at H.Q. 8th Som. L.I. at 10A.M.
on 13/6/17.

11/6/17  5 O.R. rejoined from Summer Rest Camp.

12/6/17  Lt J.J.Schooling and 7 O.R. granted leave from
12/6/17 to 22/6/17 inc. 2nd Lt P.C.Hagon Act Adj. vice
Lt A.H.Llewellyn. Sgt Cornwell H. awarded D.C.M. vide
London Gazette" King's birthday Honours.

13/6/17  2nd Lt H.O.Pring Ast. Adj. from this date.

14/6/17.  Reference D.R.O.2574 d/- 13/6/17.
The Field Marshall Commanding in Chief has under authority
granted by his Majesty the King awarded decorations
the following officers as shown below for acts of
gallantry during operations South of the River SCARPE
9/13th April 1917.
MILITARY CROSS  2nd Lt J.H.B.Gegg,
Lt F.R.Alford,   also for acts of gallantry North of
SCARPE 23/30th April 1917.
MILITARY CROSS.  Capt. J.H.M.Hardyman.
2nd Lt A/Capt M.K.F.Saunders, 2nd Lt F.R.Cooksley,

14/6/17.  Draft of 122 O.R. joined battalion.

20/6/17.  Lt F.R.Cooksley and 5 O.R. granted leave from
20/6/17 to 30/6/17 inclusive.

22/6/17.  2nd Lt C.O.Findlay, & 2nd Lt W.R.Worsley joined
battalion.

25/6/17.  2nd Lt F.A.Matthews rejoined battalion
X  2 Other Ranks proceeded to Eng as candidates for Temp. Commissn

Lt Col.
8th (S) Bn. Somerset Light Infantry.

# WAR DIARY or INTELLIGENCE SUMMARY

*(Erase heading not required.)*

Army Form C. 2118.

| Place | Date | Hour | Summary of Events and Information | Remarks and references to Appendices |
|---|---|---|---|---|
| | | | June. War Diary. 1917. | |
| | 25/6/17. | | 2 O.R. granted leave from 24/6/17 to 3/7/17 2nd Lt H.G.Ward and 1. Other Rank granted leave from 17/6/17 to 27/6/17 . | |
| | 26/6/17. | | 7 O.R. granted leave from 27/6/17 to 6/7/17 inclusive. | |
| | 26/6/17. | | 2nd Lt E.A.Matthews to Command H.Q" Coy. from this date. | |
| | 28/6/17. | | Capt R.H.E.Bennett joined Battalion . | |

[signature]
Lt Col.
8th (S) Bn. Somerset Light Infantry.

War Diary
7th Somerset
July 1917.

Vol 23

63/3722 L

## WAR DIARY July 1917.

2/7/17. Battalion was relieved in the trenches morning of the 2nd by the Gloucester Regt., and marched independently to Billets at Dranoutre. Relief being complete by noon.

10/7/17. Battalion left Dranoutre afternoon of the 10th, to relieve 10th Royal Fusiliers in the RIGHT SUPPORT TRENCHES WYTSCHAETE-MESSINES RIDGE. Battalion Headquarters being at LUMM FARM.

11/8/17. Battalion relieved 13th Royal Fusiliers in Front Line (Right). Relief being complete about midnight.

20/7/17. Battalion was relieved by 8th East Lancs Regt., and marched independently to Reserve Line East of KEMMEL HILL.

25/7/17. Battalion moved up again and relieved 8th East Lancs Regt., Headquarters being at LUMM FARM.

26/7/17. Battalion relieved by 13th Royal Fusiliers and marched back to old Line E. of KEMMEL HILL.

29/8/17. Battalion relieved 10th Royal Fusiliers in the Line, Headquarters being LUMM FARM. Relief being complete about midnight.

Major,
for Lt. Col.
8th(S) Battalion Somerset L.I.

## WAR DIARY July 1917.

| Date | |
|---|---|
| 3/7/17. | 3.O.R. wounded in action. The undermentioned Officers joined Bn this day:- 2nd Lt D.H. Cox. Lt. S. Donne. Lt. P.C. Hagon and 6.O.R. granted leave from 4/7/17 to 14/7/17 inc. |
| 5/7/17. | 2nd LT. S. Goodman granted leave from 6/7/17 inc. to 16/7/17. |
| 7/7/17. | Lt Col. D.W1C.Davies Evans having been taken on the strength of the 8th Lincs Regt. is struck off the strength (Auth. 63rd Bde. letter No 9892 dated 7/8/17.) |
| 8/7/17. | 15642 Ptr Connor J. was tried by F.G.C.M. on 3/7/17 for "When on Active Service Drunkenness", and awarded 42days F.P. No 1. |
| 9/7/17. | 19140 Pte Osborne T. awarded 28days F.P. No 1. |
| 13/7/17. | 3.O.R. proceeded to Eng as Candidates for Temp. Commission. Lt. Coll M.C.C. Miers joined Bn. and took over Command vice Lt. Col. H1K. Umfreville D.S.O1 to Base 10/7/17. The undermentioned Officers were wounded in action:- Lt. Col. M1C.C. Miers 12/8/17 Major J.G. Underwood          " 2nd Lt. H.A. de F. Ford       " Lt. A.H1 Llewellyn    13/7/17 (accidental) 2nd Lt1 A.G. Swain having been invalided to Eng. is struck off the strength. (Auth. List 817 dated 7/7/17. Major H.S.G. Richardson joined Bn. and took over Command. |
| 10/8/17. | 2.O.R. killed in action |
| 12/7/17. | 2.O.R.    "      "     " |
| 13/7/17. | 2.O.R.    "      "     " 14.O.R. wounded in action. |

Major,
for Lt. Col.

8th (S) Battalion Somerset L.I.

## WAR DIARY July 1917.

| Date | |
|---|---|
| 13/7/17. | 7.O.R. granted leave from 11/7/17 to 21/7/17 inc. |
| 15/7/17. | Captn. F.H. Baker joined Bn. |
| 14/7/17. | 2.O.R. killed in action. |
| | 1.O.R. wounded in action. |
| | 1.O.R. granted leave from 12/7/17 to 22/7/17. inc. |
| 18/7/17. | 6.O.R. joined Bn from Base. |
| 17/7/17. | 2nd Lt. H.B. Smith and 8.O.R. killed in action. |
| | 2nd Lt. C.D. Hagon, 2nd Lt. G. Durston, |
| | 2nd Lt. A.J. Crease, and 16.O.R. wounded in action. |
| 18/7/17. | 2nd Lt P.S. Bryant and 4.O.R. granted leave from 18/7/17 to 28/7/17 inc. |
| 20/7/17. | 17.O.R. jointd Bn. from Base. |
| | 2nd Lt H.K. Pople joined Bn. 18/7/17. |
| 18/7/17. | 1.O.R. wounded in action |
| 19/7/17. | 1.O.R.    "      "      " |
| 20/7/17. | 1.O.R.    "      "      " |
| | Captn J.H.M. Hardyman appointed 2nd in Command vice Major J.G. Underwood wounded 12/7/17. |
| | 30748 Cpl Clennen has been awarded the MILITARY MEDAL under Bde. letter No. 360 dated 19/7/17. Congratulations from Div. and Bde. Commanders to recipient. |
| 21/7/17. | 2nd Lt. C.A. Baird having been pronounced "P.B." by Medical Board is struck off strength. |
| 23/7/17. | 2nd Lt. P.C. Hagon to be Adj. and Temp. Lt. whilst so employed, vice Captn A.W. Phillips (Second Army Sch) 21st Nov. 1916. |
| 24/7/17. | 9.O.R. joined Bn from Base. 2nd Lt. R.P. Braund having been invalided to Eng. is struck off the strength. Captn F.C. Humphries joined Bn. |
| 26/7/17. | Lt. F.G. Hinton and Lt. A.P. Morgan rejoined Bn. |
| | 4.O.R. granted leave from 18/7/17 to 28/7/17 inc. |
| | 6.O.R.   "      "      "  25/7/17 to 4/8/17.  " |
| | 1.O.R.   "      "      "      "  25/8/17.  " |
| | 2.O.R.   "      "      "  27/7/17 "  7/8/17.  " |
| 29/7/17. | 2nd Lt. F.J. Pickford, 2nd Lt. W.H. Pickford joined Bn. |
| 30/7/17. | 2nd Lt W.V. Glanville joined Bn. |

Major for Lt. Col.
8th (S) Battalion Somerset L.I.

Wardway
8th Somersets
Aug 1917

| Place | Date | Hour | Summary of Events and Information | Remarks and references to Appendices |
|---|---|---|---|---|

## August War Diary 1917.

**29.7.17** The Battalion left Camp at East of LINDENHOEK for trenches east of LUMM FARM in O. 26 27 & 28, which it had previously occupied. The relief of the 13th Bn. Royal Fus. was carried out without incident. "A" Coy in Ridge Defence Line. "D" in Reserve Line. "C" in support and "B" in shell hole line.

**30.7.17.**
"A" "D" & "C" Coys moved up between 10 and 11 p.m. to SHELL HOLE LINE in O.29.a.& c. between GRASS FARM on Right and WAMBEEK stream on left. "B" Coy throwing out a covering party prior to the move. "D" Coy occupied shell holes just in advance of the SHELL HOLE LINE on the left, with "A" Coy in immediate support. "C" Coy in shell holes on the right.
10th Bn. Royal Fus. took over the Reserve Line. Move completed and Companies reported in assembly positions at 3.30 a.m. 31./7.17.

**31.7.17.**
3.50 a.m. Commencement of first phase by 8th Bn. Linc. Regt and 4th Bn. Middx Regt cooperating with 19th Div. on their left, in attack on RIFLE FARM.
During this phase enemy put down moderate barrage on our front line and support trenches, causing a few casualties. 2nd Lt. H.R. Kirk being severely wounded, and dying shortly afterwards.
5.0 a.m. O.C. 8th Somerset L.I. informed by Liaison Officer at Bn. H.Q. that RIFLE FARM had been carried at 4.20 a.m.
7.50 a.m. Commencement of second phase "D" Coy 8th Somerset L.I. cooperating with two companies 8th Bn. Linc. Regt on their left, with "C" Coy on their right, advanced to clear BEEK WOOD of the enemy, and to establish a new line from the WAMBEEK just S. of WAM FARM to a post to be established by 10th Bn. York & Lanc Regt South of GRASS FARM.
9.0 a.m. A/Capt Hunt returned to Battn H.Q. wounded in left arm and reported success of attack to Western outskirts of BEEK FARM enclosures and that his Company were digging in.

*Richardson Lt-Col*
*Commanding*
*8th Somerset L.I.*

| Place | Date | Hour | Summary of Events and Information | Remarks and references to Appendices |
|---|---|---|---|---|

31/7/17.

10 a.m. Pigeon report received from Capt. H.G. Baker M.C. O.C. "D" Coy that two platoons had gone forward to clear BEEK enclosures and that the remainder of his Coy were digging in on the left of "A" Coy in touch with LINCOLNS that all Officers of "A" Coy had become casualties, Capt Hunt and 2nd Lt Kirk and 2nd Lt. Adams wounded. that "A" Coy was not in touch with "C" Coy on the right but that they were visible digging in the other side of a small ridge.

1.5p.m. Report by runner from Capt. Baker that 2nd Lt. Blake "D" Coy had been killed, that the remainder of the two platoons that had gone forward had returned, that posts had been established at N.W. and S.W. corners of enclosures.

3.p.m. Report by runner from 2nd Lt. Wood "C" Coy that Capt. Baker M.C. O.C. "C" Coy had been wounded, and that he was digging in and was in touch with York and Lancs Regt on Right.

5.40p.m. Pigeon report from Capt. Baker that platoons sent forward had retired, that posts were established N and S of BEEK FARM that 2nd Lt. Blake had been killed, that his platoon had suffered many casualties and that it was at that hour impossible to bring in wounded.

About 8p.m. message received from Heavy Artillery Reserves that enemy were massing for counter attack E. of BEEK WOOD. Our guns opened and the attack did not materialise.

Captured positions consolidated during night. Coys reorganised and posts established.

"B" Coy moved up to fill gap between "A" and "C" during night from old shell hole line. "C" Coy 10th York and Lancs Regt came into that line in support of 8th Som. L.I. 1 Coy 10th Bn. R.F's in reserve under command of O.C. 8t Som. L.I.

Comparatively quiet day no counter attacks. Battn relieved by 13th Bn. R.F's after dark without incident.

1.8.17. Marched back independantly to Reserve Line East of KEMMEL staying one night and then on to Billets at DRANOUTRE, relief being complete by midnight.

8.8.17. Battalion left Dranoutte afternoon of the

H.C. Richardson Lt Col.
Commdg. 8th Somerset L.I.

| Place | Date | Hour | Summary of Events and Information | Remarks and references to Appendices |
|---|---|---|---|---|
| | | | 8th relieving 9th Bn. Cheshires in Support at IRISH HOUSE (N.23.c.8.7) relief being complete by 7p.m. | |
| | 15.8.17 | | Battalion relieved 10th Loyal N. Lancs in the Front Line Right Sub Sector night 15/16 relief being complete about 2a.m. | |
| | 21.8.17. | | Battalion relieved by 11th R. Warwicks in Front Line and returned independantly to IRISH HOUSE. Relief complete by midnight. | |
| | 26.8.17. | | The Battalion was relieved by 13th K.R.R's of 111 Bde in reserve at IRISH HOUSE the relief commencing about 11a.m.. Battalion then marched to BIRR BARRACKS East of LOCRE . | |
| | 29.8.17. | | Battalion left BIRR BARRACKS night of 29.8.17 and relieved 10th Bn. York L Lanc Regt in SPOIL BANK support Line. Bn. H.Q. I.33.c.7.8. | |

Comdg. 8th Somerset L.I. Lt Col.

31.7.17. 5 O.R. joined Battalion.
30.7.17. 2 O.R. wounded in action.
31.7.17. 2 O.R. proceeded to Eng. as candidates
         for Temp. commission.
31.7.17 6 O.R. granted leave from 1.8.17 -11.8.17
3.8.17. Congratulatory Message -:
       "My warmest congratulations to you
            personally and to Commanders, Staffs, Troops
under your command for the complete success of the
2nd Army Operations yesterday. Such a satisfactory opening to the Battle is full of promise for further and
still greater successes"
            (Sd) D. HAIG.
                    Field Marshall.
The following message dated 31st July has been
received -: from 37th Div -:"The Divl Commander
congratulates you heartily on your magnificent
fight today."
3.8.17. 4 O.R. joined Bn. -
        Casualties -:
        2nd Lt. W.R. Worsley Killed 1.8.17.
        "    H.R. Kirk      Killed   31.7.17.
        "    F.W.R. Blake   Killed   31.7.17.
        Capt. F.H. Baker Wounded 31.7.17.
        A/Capt H.J. Hunt Wounded 31.7.17.
        LT. S. Donne Wounded 31.7.17.
        2nd Lt. R.W. Adams Wounded 31.7.171
        Other ranks Killed in action   37.
Other ranks Wounded                    90.
Other ranks "W and M"                   6.
Other Ranks "Missing"                  14.
4.8.17. Maj. J.H.M. Hardyman and 1 O.R. granted
        leave 3.8.17 to 13.8.17.
6.8.17. 2nd Lt. H.J. Cuningham Joined Batt.
        Lt. H.C. Pring and 11 O.R. granted leave
        8.8.17 to 18.8.18.
9.8.17  2nd Lt. G.A. Ham and 2nd Lt. F.N. Eskell
        joined.
13.8.17 2nd Lt. W.G. Willatt granted leave from
        15.8.17 to 25.8.17.
        9 Other Ranks ditto.
14.8.17. 2nd Lt. E.A. Matthews to R.F.C. as
         Observer and struck off strength.
15.8.17. 4 O.R. wounded in action.
16.8.17 2 O.R. Killed and 8 O.R. Wounded.
17.8.17 1 O.R. Killed and 2 wounded.
18.8.17. 4 O.R. wounded in action.

            [signature] Richardson
                         Lt.Col.
        Comdg. 8th Somerset. L.I.

# WAR DIARY or INTELLIGENCE SUMMARY

| Place | Date | Hour | Summary of Events and Information | Remarks and references to Appendices |
|---|---|---|---|---|
| | | | 21.8.17. 31 O.R. Joined and 2nd Lt. W. Ward.<br>19.8.17. 2 O.R. killed in action.<br>20.8.17. 5 O.R. wounded in action.<br>22.8.17. 3 O.R. proceeded to Eng as candidates for tempy commissions.<br>22.8.17. 10 O.R. granted leave from 22.8.17 to 1.9.17. inc.<br>23.8.17 The Bde Commander congratulates the undermentioned N.C.O's and Men to whom the decorations as under have been awarded for Gallantry in the Field :-<br>15760 Sgt Ballantyne J. Bar to Military Medal.<br>15185 Sgt Carroll H. Military Medal.<br>27852 Sgt Marvin A. Military Medal.<br>17108 Cpl Seabrook E. Military Medal.<br>24922 Pte T. Rowlett Military Medal.<br>The Field Marshall Commanding in chief has under authority granted by His Majesty the King awarded the following decorations to the undermentioned Officers and N.C.O's<br>        Bar to Military Cross.<br>T/Lt. (A/Capt) H.G. Baker.<br>Conspicuous gallantry and devotion to duty E. of OOSTTAVERNE 31.7.17.<br>        MILITARY CROSS.<br>2nd Lt. (A/Capt) H.J. Hunt Ditto.<br>2nd Lt. H.K. POPLE<br>235121 L/c Hobbs G. and 7674 Sgt Wells F.<br>Awarded D.C.M. for Distinguished bravery on 31.7.17 E of OOSTTAVERNE.<br>24.8.17. 2nd Lt. C.H. Madden joined Bn.<br>25.8.17. 1 Sgt appointed 2nd Lt. and posted to 7th Bn. Som. L.I.<br>26.8.17. 2nd Lt. S. Goodman to Hospital sick.<br>26.8.17. 2nd Lt. H.K. Austin Joined Bn.<br>27.8.17. Following Officers joined :-<br>   2nd Lt. H.G. Stone    2nd Lt. H.J. Smith.<br>   " H.J. Friend.       " N.H. Crees.<br>   " G.H. Hearder      " D.A. Hill.<br>   " G.B. Brown.        "<br>27.8.17. 23 O.R. joined.<br>28.8.17. 2nd Lt. P.B. Doman joined.<br>30.8.17. 2nd Lt. F. Pfaff Joined. | |

Richards
Comdg 5th Somerset L.I. Lt Col

Army Form C. 2118.

Vol 25

War Diary
8th Somersets.
Sept 1917

September WAR DIARY 1917.

## PART I.

7/9/17.
The Battalion relieved by 10th Royal Fusiliers, and took over same billets in reserve East of KEMMEL The Battalion H.Qrs. being at IRISH HOUSE.
10/9/17.
The Battalion left IRISH HOUSE at 1 p.m. and marched to Mount KOKERLLE (M 13 b 8.9.) route via, BRULOOZE, Canada Corner, Mount Rouge, Mount Vaidagne, being in billets by 4 p.m.
19/9/17.
The Battalion left MOUNT KOKERLLE (M 13 b 8.9.) at 9-20 p.m. marching with Bde.
Battalion arrived in billets at FERMOY FARM by 11-15 p.m.
21/9/17.
The Battalion left FERMOY FARM 5 p.m., and marched to billets at Mount KOKERLLE (M 13b 8.9.) arriving 7-30 p.m.
27/9/17.
The Battalion left Camp ( M 13 b 8.9.) for the line, being conveyed in lorries, relieving the a Bn. Hants Regt.
The Transport and Stores being Brigaded proceeded to N 3 c 5.8. removing on the 29th to N 15 a 3.2.

-----------------

Major for Lt Col.
8th (S) Bn. Somerset Light Infantry.

# September WAR DIARY 1917.

## PART II.

**1/9/17.**
Draft of 10 Other Ranks joined Bn.
9 Other Ranks granted leave from 1/9/17 to 11/9/17
**2/9/17.**
1 Other rank wounded in action.
**6/9/17.**
1 Other rank accidentally wounded.
1 Other rank proceeded to Eng as candidate for Temp Commission.
2nd Lt L.J.H.White and 9 O.R. granted leave 8/9/17 to 18/9/17.
2 Other Ranks granted leave 4/9/17 to 14/9/17.
No. 6222 Pte Baker E. tried by F.G.C.M. 29/8/17 awarded 56 days F.P. No.1. for " Conduct to the prejudice of good order and military discipline. When on active service "using insubordinate language to his superior officer.
Sentence confirmed by G.O.C.63rd Bde.
**13/9/17.**
1 Other Rank to Eng. as candidate for Temp. Commission.
**14/9/17.**
2nd Lt L.C.Bodey and 8 O.R. granted leave from 15/9/17 to 25/9/17.
**15/9/17.**
2 O.R. Joined Bn.
The Following Extract from List 152 of Appoinrments Commissions Etc. dated Sept 1917 are as follows.
Temp Lt F.G.Hinton to be A/Capt whilst in command of a Coy. 15/8/17.
    The undernamed to be A/Capts (additional) dated 20th July 1917.
    Temp Lt A.P.Morgan
    Temp 2nd Lt G.A.Ham.
**22/9/17.**
The following message has been received from the G.O.C. IX Corps via G.O.C. 37th Div., and is published for information.
" I should like to thank you and the whole of your Division for the excellent and loyal work which has been done in pushing on all the preporations for the attack by the 19th Div.
    I am jidging not only from my own observations, but from the remarks and comments I have heard from all sides, specially from the 19th themselves.
    I am confident 6f their cussess, but it will be in a large measure due to the help which the 37th have given them. "
**23/9/17.**
2nd Lt H.G.Ward granted leave from 22/9/17 to
**1/10/17.**
No. 17735 L/c Wood L.S.J. (Att 63rd T.M.B.) tried by F.G.C.M. 20/9/17 for " Absenting himself without leave" found guilty and sentences to 42 days F.P.No. 1. Under arrest awaiting trial from 23/8/17. 14 days F.P.No.1. remitted and confirmed by G.O.C. 63rd Bde.

Major for Lt.Col
8th (S) Bn. Somerset Light Infantry.

| Place | Date | Hour | Summary of Events and Information | Remarks and references to Appendices |
|---|---|---|---|---|
| | | | 26/9/17.<br>Lt E.N. Eskell appointed Officer in charge of Battn. Physical Training and Bayonet Fighting.<br>2nd Lt C.H. Madden appointed Officer in charge of Anti Gas training.<br><br>1 C.Q.M.S. proceeded to Eng. as candidate for Temp. Commission.<br>25/9/17.<br>Draft of 38 Other Ranks joined Bn.<br><br><br><br>[signature]<br>Major for Lt Col.<br>8th (S) Bn. Somerset Light Infantry. | |

War Diary
6th Somersets.

Oct 1917

WAR DIARY for OCTOBER 1917.

PART II.
--------

1/10/17.
2/Lt W.Wood. and 3 Other ranks granted leave from
29/9/17 to 10/10/17.

2/10/17.
"Wounded"  2/Lt W.V.Glanville and 3 Other ranks.

3/10/17.
"Wounded" (Gas)  2/Lt D.A.Hill.
1 Other rank granted leave from 29/9/17 to
10/10/17 incl.

4/10/17.
The following Officers were "Killed in Action"

    Capt.  F.C.Humphreys. M.C.
    2/Lt   H.J.Smith.
    2/Lt   H.J.Friend.
27 Other Ranks were "Killed in Action"
same date.
The following were "Wounded in Action"

    Lt(A/Capt.)  F.G.Hinton.
    2/Lt         W.H.Wickard.
    2/Lt         E.N.Eskell.
and 72 Other ranks.
2 Other ranks "Wounded at duty"
12 Other ranks reported "Missing".

6/10/17.
9 Other ranks granted leave from 6/10/17 to
16/10/17 incl.

8/10/17.
A Draft of 47 Other ranks joined Battalion.

4/10/17.
A Draft of 53 Other Ranks arrived at 63rd Bde
School and joined Battalion 10/10/17.

10/10/17.
Hon.Lt. & Qr.Mr. J.J.Schooling granted leave from
10/10/17 to 20/10/17 incl.

10/10/17.
Extract from London Gazette, dated October 6th 1917.

The following Temp. Second Lieuts. to be
Temp. Lieutenants. (July 1st )

| | | |
|---|---|---|
| H.J.Cuningham, | D.H.Cox, | D.J.L.Routh, |
| V.L.Plant. | E.H.Morgan. | A.F.Webb. |
| E.A.Matthews, | G.A.Ham, | P.C.Hagon. |
| E.N.Eskell. | F.G.Adlam. | V.G.Willatt. |

                                            Major.
Commdg. 8th (S) Bn. Somerset Light Infy.

(2).

| Place | Date | Hour | Summary of Events and Information | Remarks and references to Appendices |
|---|---|---|---|---|
| | | | 10/10/17.
Major The Hon: R.T.St John crossposted to the 8th Lincoln Regt, and took over Command vice Lt.Col D.W.C.Davies Evans to Eng.

2/Lt H.G.Ward to England on 6 months tour of duty, (Authy: W.O.Letter, 121/France/ 937 ( M.S.I.R.) dated 13/9/17, 121/France/ 1957 (M.S.K.) dated 19/9/17.
One Other rank Killed in Action.

11/10/17.
1 O.R. "Killed" and 7 O.R. "Wounded"

14/10/17.
1 O.R. "Killed" and 20 O.R. "Wounded".

15/10/17.
2/Lt L.P.E.Doman and 2/Lt C.O.Findlay , 6 O.R. "Wounded" in action.

13/10/17.
7 Other ranks granted leave from 13/10/17 to 23/10/17 incl.

15/10/17.
Major J.H.M.Hardyman appointed 2nd in Command from 10/10/17 vice Major The Hon: R.T.St John, posted 8th Lincoln Regt.

17/10/17.
2/Lt N.H.Crees to Command "C" Company from 5/10/17 vice Lt.(A/Capt.) F.G.Hinton. "Wounded"

20/10/17.
Lt Colonel H.S.C.Richardson granted leave from 20/10/17 to 30/10/17

19/10/17.
Draft of 56 Other Ranks joining Battalion.

21/10/17.
Lt V.L.Plent appointed Battalion Intelligence, Musketry and Sniping Officer.

24/10/17.
2/Lt W.Deeming, joined Battalion.

Major.
Commdg. 8th (S) Bn. Somerset Light Infy. | |

(3).

24/10/17.

The Corps, Division and Brigade Commanders congratulate the undermentioned N.C.O's and men to whom decorations as under have been awarded for gallantry in the Field.

No. 15674 Sgt W. HEDLEY.   For most conspicuous gallantry and devotion to duty EAST of YPRES on October 4th 1917.

No. 19096 Pte A. MARTIN.   For conspicuous gallantry, determination and devotion to duty EAST of YPRES on October 4th. 1917.

No. 15469 Cpl H. WALKER.   For conspicuous gallantry and devotion to duty on October 4th. 1917.

No. 16123 L/c H. EVIS.   For conspicuous gallantry and devotion to duty on October 4th. 1917.

No. 21808 Cpl E. LACEY.   For gallantry and devotion to duty on October 4th 1917.

--------------------------------

Major.
Commdg. 8th (S) Bn. Somerset Light Infantry.

(4).

## WAR DIARY for OCTOBER 1917.

### PART I.

**5/10/17.**
The Battalion was relieved by xxxx a Battn. of Bedford Regt in trenches, embussing at BUSS CORNER arriving at FERMOY FARM about 6 a.m. on 6/10/17.

**10/10/17.**
The Battalion left FERMOY FARM at 3 p.m. for the trenches, relieving 6th Bn. Bedford Regt, in the Front line, Right Sub-Sector ( BASSEVILLEBEEK)
The Battn. proceeded in buses as far as SPOIL BANK from here by sections with intervals of 200 yds.
Rear Battn. H.Qrs being at BEAVER CAMP (N.15.a.4.2.)

**15/10/17.**
37th Division relieved by 39th Division.
The Battalion embussing at SPOIL BANK arrived at FRONTIER CAMP (M.13.b.8.9.) about midnight, being relieved by a Battalion of the Royal Sussex Regt.

**21/10/17.**
The Battalion left Camp at M.13.b.8.9. at 8-35 a.m. and marched to MOOLENACKER, via, BERTHAN, SCHAEXKEN, METEREN. Distance about 8 miles, arrived in billets by 3 p.m.

**29/10/17.**
The Battalion plus one Coy. of 8th Lincoln Regt. embussed from MOOLENACKER at 10-30 a.m. for Camp at I.3.b. (1600 yds East of YPRES) for the purpose of road making and repairing.
Battalion Transport and Details remaining at MERRIS.

Major.
Commdg. 8th (S) Bn. Somerset Light Infantry.

(5).

## WAR DIARY for October 1917.

### OPERATIONS    OCTOBER 4TH 1917.

With reference to operations in which this Battalion took part on 4th October 1917 is as follows.

This Battalion attacked at Zero, advancing its centre and left on to its first objective, the right of the line being already far enough forward. This operation employed two companies.

The barrage was falling mostly beyond the objective, so there was no question of getting close up behind it

The enemy was found to occupy a series of strong points North and South of the Strong point at J.27.a.05.05.

This line was just East of the high ground which was our objective and was practically on the same level. Immediately the Coys. appeared on the crest line they were received by machine gun and rifle fire. They reached their objective by sectional rushes and attempted to consolidate under intense machine gun fire from J 27.a.05.05. and 3 machine guns 450 yards away on the right flank at J.27.c.central.

These latter machine guns were known previously and it was hoped that the flank barrage would keep them quiet, this however was not the case.

Immediately the front Companies reached their objective, the enemy started local bombing counter attacks. His bombers wore no equipment, and each threw two stick grenades simultaneously.

Our posts did not withdraw but were almost wiped out by bombs and machine gun fire, a large gap occurring between the 8th Lincoln Regt and ourselves.

Major J.H.M. Hardyman M.C. at once moved up a Lewis gun to fill this gap at the same time reinforcing the objective line, while 2/Lt N.H.Crees led a most gallant attack upon the strong point at J 27.a.05.05. (At night 2/Lt N.H.Crees brought back the 3 survivors of this attack, having remained all day in shell-holes close to the strong point, during which time 2/Lt Crees twice had his bayonet broken by bombs while firing on the enemy).

Major Hardyman then saw the 8th Lincoln Regt. withdraw on the left, and therefore decided that it was imperative to retain sufficient men to hold our original line at all costs.

After he had set these aside he planned a second attack upon J.27.a.05.05. to be undertaken by 2/Lt Smith, 2 Lewis Gun Teams and 20 men, at the same time reinforcing the objective line and right flank with the Reserve Company.

2/Lt H.J.Smith was killed while most gallantly leading this attack, and none of the party were able to reach the strong point.

Major.
Commdg. 8th (S) Bn. Somerset Light Infantry.

(6).

OPERATIONS. (Continued)..

Meanwhile on the right flank a strong post was dug in advance of the posts previously held by the right Company. This was successfully held against repeated bombing attacks. On the left and centre, 2/Lt Pickard who had been sent up with reinforcements, withdrew the only 2 men remaining unwounded, having resisted enemy invitations to surrender and himself being wounded twice.

Major.
Commdg. 8th (S) Bn. Somerset Light Infantry.

## WAR DIARY for November 1917.

The Battalion plus one Coy 10th York and Lancaster Regt. having completed the tour of working parties in the area East of YPRES, being incamp at I.3.b. and being relieved by a Battalion of Rifle Brigade on November 6th 1917. proceeded to the MERRIS area by lorries, arriving in billets about 8 p.m.

The Battalion left MERRIS area for BIRR BARRACKS (LOCRE) at 8.10 a.m., marched via BAILLEUL, arriving in huts (BIRR BARRACKS) about 11.30 a.m. 9/11/17.

Nov 10th The battalion left BIRR BARRACKS at 8.15 a.m. enroute for MOATED GRANGE CAMP (O.1.a.6.3.) Sheet 28.S.W.) arriving about 11.30 a.m. Route. via DRULOOZE - KEMMEL - VIERSTRAAT - BRASSERIE -
The Quartermaster Stores and Transport being at BEDFORD CAMP at (N.20.b.4.8.)

The unit left MOATED GRANGE CAMP (O.1.a.) at 1.45 p.m. for TOURNAI Camp at N.10.b.80.45. taking over from 13th Royal Fusiliers. 17/11/17.
While the Brigade was in Support, the unit supplied working parties in the front line and carrying for R.E's. Salvage was collected from the forward area and brought from the forward area also in the close vicinity of the Camp

The battalion moved into the front line from TOURNAI CAMP 25/11/17 and relieved 13th Bn. Rifle Bde. in left sub-section.
Companies entrained at BARDENBROUG SIDING N.3.c.2.4. and proceeded to ESSEX SIDING (I.28.b.) where guides met the battalion enroute for Front Line.
Battalion Headquarters being in THE GLEN

8th (S) Bn. Somerset Light Infantry.

(2)

14/1/17.
    Two N.C.O's proceeded to England as candidates for Temp. Commissions.

16/11/17.
    Twelve Other Ranks granted leave from 16/11/17 to 1/12/17.

    2nd Lt W.T.HUCKER joined the battalion 16/11/17.

20/11/17.
    Two N.C.O's proceeded to England as candidates for Temp Commission.
    Three Privates proceeded to England as Skilled ploughmen.

21/11/17.
    Nineteen Other Ranks joined the battalion.

26/11/17.
    Capt. H.PIKE was a member of a Field General Court martial assembling at the Headquarters 63rd M.G. Coy. on Monday 26th inst.

24/11/17.
    No. 9004 C.S.M. Henman W. gazetted to to 1st Bn. Gloucestershire Regt as 2nd Lieut.

23/11/17.
    One Private "Killed in action" 23/11/17.

    Thirteen Other Ranks granted leave to England from 23/11/17 to 8/12/17.

8th (S) Bn. Somerset Light Infantry.

PART II.
--------

1/11/17.
The Field Marshal Commanding-in-Chief has under authority granted by His Majesty the King awarded the following decorations to the undernamed.

THE MILITARY CROSS.

T/Lt(A/Capt.) F.G.HINTON.   For conspicuous gallantry and resourceful leadership East of YPRES on 4th October 1917.

THE DISTINGUISHED CONDUCT MEDAL.

No.14779 Sgt E.DYER.   For conspicuous gallantry, determination and devotion to duty, East of YPRES 4/10/17.

No.27859 Sgt W.DAVIES.   For conspicuous gallantry, determination and devotion to duty, East of YPRES 4/10/17.

No.19701 Pte Taylor B.A.   For conspicuous gallantry and devotion to duty East of YPRES on the 13th and 14th October 1917.

7/11/17.
Three N.C.O's proceeded to England as candidates for Temp. Commission.

8/11/17.
2nd Lt W.Deeming and 4 other ranks granted leave from 30/10/17 to 9/11/17 incl.

10/11/17.
Capt P.C.Hagon and 12 other ranks granted leave from 10/11/17 to 24/11/17.

A/Capt. A.P.Morgan was selected for temporary duty as O.C. No. 18 Prisoner of War Coy. from 10/11/17.

2nd Lt H.K.Pople appointed temporary command of "B" Coy. from 10/11/17.

12/11/17.
Two N.C.O's proceeded to England as candidates for Temp.Commission.

13/11/17.
The Divisional Commander has written expressing his extreme gratification at the good salvage work done by the 8th Somerset L.I. when at ST JEAN Camp near YPRES.

8th (S) Bn. Somerset Light Infantry.

WAR DIARY for December 1917.

7/12/17.
The following extract from List No. 167 of Appointments, Commissions etc. dated 12/11/17 is as follows:-

    2nd Lt L.J.H.WHITE   to be A/Capt.  12th Oct. 17.
    2nd Lt N.H.Crees.    to be A/Capt.  25th Oct. 17.

8/12/17.
2nd Lt H.K.Pople and 13 Other ranks were granted leave to England from 8/12/17 to 22/12/17 incl.

Lt.Col. S.S.Jenkyns joined the Battalion 7/12/17 and took over Temp. Command vice Lt.Col. H.S.C.Richardson A/Brigade Commander, 63rd Infantry Brigade.

13/12/17.
One N.C.O. proceeded to England as candidate for temporary Commission.
Five Other Ranks proceeded to Eng. on leave from 14/12/17 to 28/12/17 incl.

Capt A.P.Morgan and 9 other ranks were granted leave to Eng. from 15/12/17 to 29/12/17 incl.

18/12/17.
Five Other ranks joined the battalion from IX Corps Reinforcement Camp 18/12/17.

One N.C.O. proceeded to Eng. as candidate for Temp. Commission.

20/12/17.
Extract London Gazette. Times 19th Dec.1917.
The King has been pleased to approve of the award of the VICTORIA CROSS to the following Officers and Other ranks.
8th (S) Bn. Somerset Light Infantry.

No. 33316 Pte T.H.Sage.

    For most conspicuous bravery during an attack on an enemy strong post. He was in a shell hole with 8 other men, one of whom was shot while in the act of throwing a bomb. The live bomb fell into the shell hole, and Private Sage, with great courage and presence of mind, immediately threw himself on it, thereby undoubtedly saving the lives of his comrades though he himself sustained very severe wounds.

*S S Jenkyns* Lt Col
8th (S) Bn. Somerset Light Infantry

WAR DIARY for December 1917.

PART I.

The Battalion on being relieved in the left sub-section returned to TOURNAI CAMP (Confusion Corner N.19.b.XXX 2.4.) on the night of 5th/6th December.
Being in support to the Brigade in the line working parties were found for the first 8 days, the remaining time being spent in training and improving the camp generally.

The Battalion proceeded to the line from TOURNAI CAMP and took over the right sub-section ( East of Hollebeke) relieving the 10th Bn. Royal Fusiliers on the night 21th/22nd Dec.
Entraining at BARDENBRUG Siding and detraining at SPOIL BANK.

On night of 29th/30th Dec. the battalion was relieved in right sub-section by 6th Bn. Bedford Regt. and proceeded to Ridge Wood taking over ALPHA BETA CAMP.
While at ALPHA BETA CAMP the battalion found working parties daily in the forward area, being in support to the Brigade in the line.

8th (S) Bn. Somerset Light Infantry.

Extract London Gazette, Times Dec 18th 1917.

Mentioned in Sir Douglas Haig's Dispatch, Nov 7th 1917.

8th (S) Bn. Somerset Light Infantry.

    Lt.Col.  H.S.C.Richardson.

    Major.  J.H.M.Hardyman  M.C.

    Lieut.  C.W.Tubbs.  M.C.

20/12/17.
    2nd Lt F.H.Pickard and 2 other ranks granted leave to England from 21/12/17 to 3/1/18.

    Extract London Gazette. dated 28/12/17.

    The undernamed to be Temp. Captains.

| | | | |
|---|---|---|---|
| Lt A/Capt. | F.G.Hinton. | 15/8/17. |
| Lt A/Capt. | H.G.Baker | " |
| Lt A/Capt. | A.P.Morgan. | 5/10/17. |
| T/Lt & Adj. | P.C.Hagon. | 15/8/17. |

Ten Other Ranks joined the Battalion from IX Corps Reinforcement Camp 20/12/17.

27/12/17.

    Four N.C.O's proceeded to England as candidates for temporary Commission.

    2nd Lt. W.L.WARD   "Killed in action" 22/12/17.

    2nd Lt. W.T.Hucker. "Wounded in action" 22/12/17.
                    Died of Wounds, 23/12/17.
    One Other rank "Wounded in action" 22/12/17.
    " " " " " " 25/12/17.

    Two Other ranks "Killed in action" and two other ranks "Wounded in action" 26/12/17.

    Six Other ranks transferred to Tank Corps
                                             14/12/17.
Thirteen Other ranks proceeded on leave to Eng. from 22/1/17 to 4/1/18.
Four Other Ranks proceeded to Eng. on leave from 28/12/17 to 11/1/18.
Lt P.H.R.Bennett and 9 other ranks proceeded to Eng. on leave from 29/12/17 to 12/1/18.

8th (S) Bn. Somerset Light Infantry.

63rd Brigade.
37th Division.

8th BATTALION

THE SOMERSET LIGHT INFANTRY.

JANUARY 1918

WAR DIARY for January 1918.

PART 1.

The Battalion left "Alpha Beta" Camp (Ridge Wood) at 3p.m. 5/1/18 arriving at "Parret" Camp at 4 p.m. 5/1/18 being releived by the 8th East Lancashire Regt and releiving the 10th Bn Royal Fusiliers.

The Battalion left "Parret" Camp at 11.30 a.m. 11/1/18 arriving at DICKEBUSCH at 1 p.m. being releived by the 13th Bn Royal Fusiliers.

The Battalion left DICKEBUSCH at 10 a.m. on 16/1/18 arriving at "Forrester" Camp at 11.30 a.m.

The Battalion was releived by the 8th Bn East Lancaster Regt at "Forrester" Camp at 11.15 a.m., marched to DICKEBUSCH, and entrained for LYNDE, arriving there at 5 p.m. and releiving the 11th Royal Warwicks.

Lt.Col. Comdg.
8th(B) Bn. Somerset Light Infantry.

PART 11

Capt. J.C.PEARD joined the Battalion 30/12/17
2/Lt. R.H.BUTTON    "     "     "     "
2/LT. J.P.HEWITT    "     "     "     "

5/1/18.
    2/Lt. J.A.Radford and 15 Other Ranks granted Leave to England from 6/1/18 to 20/1/18

8/1/18.
    Ten Other Ranks joined the Battalion.

9/1/18.
    One N.C.O. proceeded to England as Candidate for Temporary Commission.

10/1/18.
    Lt.V.L.Plant and 4 Other Ranks were granted Leave to England from 11/1/18 to 25/1/18.

4/1/18.
    The following Officers joined the Battalion 4/1/18.
        2/Lt. W.E.HAYES      )
        2/Lt. H.A. DRAKEFORD ) :- Devon Regt.
        2/Lt. P.J. JONES.    )
            and 2/Lt. S.T.DYTE.

6/1/18.
    2/Lt. C.H.Madden and 13 Other Ranks were granted Leave to England from 7/1/18 to 21/1/18.
    One Other Rank was granted One Months Leave to England from 7/1/18 to 7/2/18.

8/1/18.
    New Honours Gazette.
    The King has been pleased to approve Awards for Distinguished Service in the Field. (Dated Jan 1st 1918) 8th (S) Btn Somerset L.I.
DISTINGUISHED CONDUCT MEDAL.      No.14856 C.S.M.Brake E.

MERITORIOUS SERVICE MEDAL.        No. 9428 A/C.S.M.Lang F.

15/1/18.
    2/Lt. H.K.Austin and 13 Other Ranks were granted to England from 15/1/18 to 29/1/18.

16/1/18
    Capt.A.P.MORGAN detained by Medical Board in England whilst on leave.
    (Authy:-37th Divl letter No. 24/1143 A.d/-15/1/18.

                        *[signature]*
                        Lt.Col.
            Comdg. 8th (S) Bn Somerset L.I.

PART 11 Contd.

16/1/18
    Lt.Col. S.S.JENKYNS. was granted Leave to England from 15/1/18 to 29/1/18.

    Capt H.G.BAKER M.C. and 4 Other Ranks were granted Leave to England from 17/1/18 to 31/1/18.

22/1/18
    Eleven Other Ranks were granted Leave to England from 22/1/18 to 5/2/18.

    Eleven Other Ranks were granted Leave to England from 23/1/18 to 6/2/18.

    Eighty Five Other Ranks joined the Battalion.

24/1/18.
    Six Other Ranks were granted Leave to England from 24/1/18 to 7/2/18.

25/1/18.
    Nine Other Rank granted Leave to England from the 29/1/18 to 12/2/18.

26/1/18.
    Lt. D.K.S.HUNT joined the Battalion.

28/1/18
    Lt. H.J.CUNNINGHAM transferred to England (Sick 30/1/18. (Authy O.C. 5/ B.R.C.H.)

29/1/18.
    One N.C.O. to England as Candidate for Temporary Commission.

    2/Lt J.LOCKE (Devon Regt) and Thirty other ranks joined the Battalion.

    Fifteen Other Ranks were granted Leave to England from 30/1/18 to 13/2/18.

                                                        Lt. Col.
                  Comdg. 8th (S) Somerset Light Infantry.

PART 11 Contd

25/1/18.
The under-mentioned were presented with Medal Ribbands by General Sir W.S. BIRDWOOD K.C.B., K.C.S.I., K.C.M.G., C.I.E., D.S.O., A.D.C. at WISQUES.

| | | |
|---|---|---|
| M.C. | Lt.& Quartermaster J.J.SCHOOLING. | For devotion to Duty. |
| M.S.M. | No.9426 C.S.M. LANG F. | For devotion to Duty. |
| M.M. | No.15674 C.S.M. Hedley W. | Conspicuous gallantry. |
| M.M. | No.15105 C.S.M. Cornwell H. | Great gallantry in Action. |
| M.M. | No.17108 Sgt. Seabrook E. | Gallantry in Action. |
| M.M. | No. 27852 A/C.Q.M.S. Marvin A.F. | Gallantry in Action. |
| D.C.M. | No.235121 Cpl.Hobbs G. | Gallantry and devotion to Duty. |
| M.M. | No. 16934 Pte Rowley W. | Conspicuous gallantry. |
| D.C.M. | No.19701 Pte Taylor B.A. | Conspicuous gallantry. |
| D.C.M. | No.27644 Sgt.Dolling F. | Most conspicuous gallantry. |

26/1/18.
Major General H.B.Williams C.B.,D.S.O. commanding 37th Division and Brig.General E.L.Challoner D.S.O. commanding 63rd Brigade inspected the Battalion.

Lt.Col.Comdg.
8th (S) Bn Somerset Light Infantry.

63rd Brigade.
37th Division.

8th BATTALION

THE SOMERSET LIGHT INFANTRY.

FEBRUARY 1918

WAR DIARY
for
February 1918.

PART 1.

14/2/18
The Battalion left BLARINGHEM AREA for the FORWARD AREA on 14/2/18. Entrained at EBLINGHEM at 9 a.m. and detrained at DICKEBUSCH at 12:30 p.m. The Battalion then proceeded by march to SCOTTISH WOOD and stayed there for one night.

15/2/18
The Battalion moved up into the front Line (Right Sub-section J.20.d.20.75L. relieving 7th Bn. Somerset Light Infantry on the night 15/16th February.

21/2/18
The Battalion moved back into support at CANADA TUNNELS, MOUNT SORREL K (I.30.b.1.3.) being relieved from Front Line by 4th Bn. Middlesex Regt. The Battalion had four casualties during their tour in the Front Line.

23/2/18
The Battalion moved back into Reserve at SCOTTISH WOOD being relieved from CANADA TUNNELS by the 8th Bn. Lincoln Regt.

25/2/18
The Battalion moved up into CANADA TUNNELS (Support) relieving the 8th Bn Lincolnshire Regt.

26/2/18                PART 11
One Other Rank was wounded.

25/2/18
Lt. & Qr Mr. D.G. CAMPBELL joined the Battalion.

26/2/18
Regt. Sergt Major Hanley J. No. 3744 joined the Battalion from 11th Bn Royal Warwicks.

27/2/18
Lt. T.S. BUSTARD (A.S.C.) joined the Battalion.

P.W.R. Bennet.    A/Adj for Lt. Colonel.
8th (S) Bn. Somerset Light Infantry.

## PART. 11.

**1/2/18**
The Battalion being in the Training Area, (BLARINGHEM) and Billited in LYNDE, training was carried out daily. Sports, football &c. and recreational training came into the programme of the week.
Inspections, route marching, tactical schemes, and musketry with range practices being some of the prominent subjects carried out.
Brigade and Battalion Competitions were arranged and the results of the Brigade Competitions were as follows:-
Transport Driving Competition...1st 8th Somerset L.I.
(The best individual Driver being No.15223,
Pte Wakefield F.)
Scouting Competition............1st 8th Somerset L.I.
Signalling Competition..........1st 8th Somerset L.I.
Lewis Gun Competition...........1st 8th Somerset L.I.

**4/2/18**
Honours and Awards
The award of the following decoration (Belgian) has been approved of by His Majesty the King.

BELGIAN CROIX DU GUERE
No. 9428 Sgt.(A/CSM) Lang F.
No.32224 Pte. Gamblin F. (Attd.63rd T.M.B.)

**5/2/18**
Lt.H.O.PRING, 2/Lt. C.H.HEARDER, and eleven other ranks were granted leave to U/K.

**7/2/18**
No.9155 Sgt.Hulbert J.H. posted to 2nd Bn Wiltshire Regt as 2/Lieut. (Authy A.G. 2158/782 (o) d/- 3/2/18.)

**12/2/18**
Lt. J.J.CRESSWELL (A.S.C), 2/Lt. A.OWEN and thirty other Ranks joined the Battalion.

**23/2/18**
Lt. D.K.S.HUNT proceeded to England (Grantham) on Machine Gun Course.

**18/2/18**
Three Other Ranks were wounded, and one of them died of wounds the same day.

**19/2/18**
One N.C.O. was wounded accidentally.

**12/2/18**
Lt.& Qr.Mr. J.J.SCHOOLING and fifteen Other Ranks were granted Leave to # U/K.

**19/2/18**
Lt. V.C.WILLATT and Twenty three Other Ranks were granted leave to U/K.

**23/2/18**
Lt. F.R.COOKSLEY M.C. proceeded to England on Six Months tour of duty.(Authy 63rd Bde Wire S.C.182 d/-23/2/18.

**24/2/18**
Three Other Ranks were granted Leave to U/K.

**26/2/18**
Lt.H.PIKE and Twenty Other Ranks were granted leave to U/K.

P.W.R.Bennett.    Lt.A/Adj. for Lt.Colonel.
8th (S) Bn.Somerset Light Infantry.

63rd Brigade.
37th Division.

8th BATTALION

THE SOMERSET LIGHT INFANTRY

MARCH 1 9 1 8

# WAR DIARY
## FOR
### MARCH 1918

| | Place | Date | Hour | Summary of Events and Information | Remarks and references to Appendices |
|---|---|---|---|---|---|

## PART 1.

**1.3.18**
The Battalion moved up into the Front Line relieving the 4th Bn. Middlesex Regiment.

**5.3.18**
The Battalion moved back to CANADA TUNNELS (Support) being relieved from the Front Line by the 8th Bn. Lincolnshire Regt. The Battalion had four casualties during this tour. (2 Killed and 2 Wounded)

**6.3.18**
One Company ("B" Coy) moved back to SCOTTISH WOOD to prepare for a Raid.

**8.3.18**
"B" Company suddenly ordered to rejoin the Battalion in CANADA TUNNELS (Support.)

**9.3.18**
The Battalion moved back to SCOTTISH WOOD being relieved from CANADA TUNNELS by the 8th Bn. Lincolnshire Regt.

**12.3.18**
The Battalion had Seven casualties whilst on Working Parties (All wounded)

**15.3.18**
The Battalion moved up into the Front Line relieving the 8th Bn. Lincolnshire Regt.

**19.3.18**
A raid was carried out by "B" Company on the night of 18th/19th, the objective being GENERAL'S DUGOUT opposite JULIA TRENCH. Two Officers (2/Lt. H.A. Drakeford and 2/Lt. Button) and 57 Other Ranks were engaged.
The scheme was to advance after a brief but intense Bombardment, enter the Dugout and seize any prisoners or documents, at the same time silencing and securing if possible any Machine Guns which were in the neighbourhood.
A Tree by the Dugout suspected to be an Observation Post was to be blown up.
Zero hour was at 2.30 a.m.
There was an intense Bombardment for five minutes by Artillery, Trench Mortars and Machine Guns, during which the raiding party formed up outside our trench (JULIA Trench).
At Zero plus 5 the Bombardment lifted and the Party made for GENERAL'S DUGOUT. This was found to be unoccupied and in Ruins. The enemy was seen running away but none were secured. The Tree was successfully blown up.
A Bombing Party advanced against a Machine Gun on the left, but was prevented from reaching it by thick wire.
The Party accordingly returned. The Whole raid was over by Zero plus 20.
The only casualty was One (Slightly Wounded) before starting.
Dummy figures were successfully used on the flanks to draw Machine Gun Fire.

Major for Lt. Colonel
6th (S) Bn Somerset Light Infy.

| | |
|---|---|
| Place | |
| | PART 1 Contd.<br>*********** |
| Date | |
| | 21.3.18<br>The Battalion moved back to CANADA TUNNELS (Support) being relieved from the Front Line by the 4th Bn.Middlesex Regiment. The Battalion had 29 (Twenty Nine) casualties during this tour, (4 Killed and 25 wounded) |
| Hour | 27.3.18<br>The Battalion moved back from CANADA TUNNELS to billets in the METEREN AREA, and stayed there for two nights. |
| | 29.3.18<br>The Battalion entrained at CAESTRE at 2 p.m. en route for the ANCRE front. |
| | 30.3.18<br>The Battalion detrained at MONDICOURT about 8 a.m. and then proceeded by march to Billets at GRENAS, staying there for one night. |
| | 31.3.18<br>The Battalion moved to HENU, being billeted there for one night. |
| | ***************<br>PART 11<br>******* |
| | 3.3.18<br>Seventy One Other Ranks joined the Battalion. |
| | 6.3.18<br>Lt.& Qr.Mr. D.G.CAMPBELL and Sixteen Other Ranks were granted leave to the United Kingdom.<br><br>Thirty Other Ranks joined the Battalion.<br><br>2/Lieut R.A.FORREST joined the Battalion. |
| Summary of Events and Information | 8.3.18<br>The undernamed Officers transferred from 10th Bn. York & Lancaster Regt. to 8th Bn Somerset Light Infantry.<br>2/Lieut K.G.WOODMANSEY and 2/Lieut A.E.GOAD. |
| | 9.3.18<br>Lt.Colonel H.S.C.RICHARDSON granted leave to the United Kingdom for the period of One month. |
| | 10.3.18<br>Capt (A/Major) S.S.JENKYNS temporarily attached to 8th (S) Bn Somerset Light Infantry. |
| | 13.3.18<br>2/Lieut W.DEMMING and Eleven Other Ranks were granted leave to the United Kingdom. |
| | 14.3.18<br>HONOURS AND AWARDS<br>The Corps Commander under Authority delegated to him, has awarded the MILITARY MEDAL to the undermentioned man.<br>No.15914. Pte WILLIS.G. 8th Somerset Light Infy.<br><br>Major for Lt.Col.<br>8th (S) Bn Somerset Light Infy. |

PART 11 Contd.
***************

**12.3.18**
The undernamed Officers posted to the 8th Bn Somerset Light Infantry from 10th Bn York & Lancaster Regt.
2/Lt. H.A.WALSH. M.C.
2/Lt. B.W.GAUNT.            )
2/Lt. S.F.STEARS            )   Attd 63rd Bde T.M.B.

**19.3.18**
Lieut D.H.COX granted Leave to the United Kingdom.

**20.3.18**
Eleven Other Ranks granted Leave to the United Kingdom.

**19.3.18**
Ten Other Ranks joined the Battalion.

**21.3.18**
Capt. P.C.HAGON proceeded to England on Six Months tour of duty at Home.

**23.3.18**
Four Other Ranks joined the Battalion.

**26.3.18**
Lt.& Qr.Mr.J.J.SCHOOLING M.C. proceeded to England on Six months tour of Duty at home.

Three Other Ranks joined the Battalion.

**24.3.18**
No.9428 A/CSM Lang F. proceeded to Base for transfer to England on Six Months tour of duty at home.

**27.3.18**
Seven Other Ranks joined the Battalion.


Major for Lt.Colonel.
8th (S) Bn Somerset Light Infantry.

63rd Brigade.
37th Division.

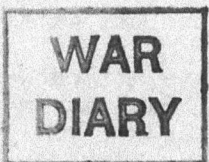

8th BATTALION

THE SOMERSET LIGHT INFANTRY

APRIL 1918

| Place | Date | Hour | Summary of Events and Information | Remarks and references to Appendices |

WAR DIARY
-for-
APRIL 1918:
**********

PART 1
------

1.4.18.

    The Battalion left HENU and proceeded by March to the Front Line (K.6.d.7.3.) relieving the 2/4th Bn. K.O.Y.L.I. and 2/4th York and Lancs Regt.

5.4.18.

    The Battalion carried out an Attack S.E. of GOMME-COURT.
    The assembly for this attack was made most difficult owing to heavy rain, darkness, and the very muddy state of the trenches.
    One Company took four hours to move from its trenches to the assembly position and had to move forward to the attack shortly after arrival.

    There was some hesitation at ZERO hour among the leading Companies, owing to the non-appearance of six expected Tanks. This caused the leading wave to somewhat lose the barrage, which however, failed to touch the first objective on the front allotted to this battalion, all the shells bursting beyond it. The first objective was reached and captured with little resistance from the enemy in a heavy mist, many enemy were found here and about 60 prisoners taken.

    The second wave leap frogged the first and continued towards the second objective, no real resistance being encountered until the line of the Western edge of ROSSIGNOL WOOD was reached, here, heavy fighting commenced, the enemy opening heavy rifle and Machine Gun fire especially from ROSSIGNOL WOOD, on the right of which our attack was definitely held up and made little further progress during the action, owing chiefly to lack of cover, and to the fact that the enemy was firing from concealed positions from within the wood.

    The left Company under Capt J.C. PEARD entered the Wood on the left and forced its way forward capturing some prisoners and machine guns, and eventually established its left close to the second objective. The right Company however had failed to enter its portion of the Wood and therefore failed to to keep touch with the left, and owing to the thickness of undergrowth and trees, it was a little time before Capt PEARD grasped the situation.

                                    Lt.Col.
    Comdg. 8th (S) Bn Somerset Light Infantry.

PART 1 Contd.
--------------

On doing so however, he immediately threw back his
right flank and endeavoured to get touch with the right
Company, gradually bringing up his line in the centre.
He met with considerable resistance from the enemy who
occupied this portion of the Wood strongly, and who put
up a most determined resistance.

Touch was not obtained with the right Company which
had been held further back, and while in this position
the left Company was heavily counter attacked by enemy
bombing parties and machine guns, which however, failed
to di-slodge them. They were then shelled, and owing to
casualties, the extended state of his line, running out
of bombs and lack of reinforcements, Captain PEARD
realised that his position was becoming untenable.

He therefore arranged covering parties and withdrew
to the left flank of the wood, occupying the Hook Trench.
Here, he re-organised, collected more bombs and forced his
way forward again to the edge of the Wood, but owing to
further casualties was unable to make progress and was
holding the HOOK TRENCH at the end of the day, having
obtained touch with the 112th Brigade who were a considerable
distan-ce away on his left.

The right Company during this time repeatedly
endeavoured to get forward but failed to do so and
suffered very heavy casualties.

The enemy counter attacked later under cover of
machine gun and bombs, and himself suffered heavily from
Rifle and Lewis Gun fire brought to bear from our first
objective. He however, surrounded the survivors on the
left of the left company, close to the wood, and captured
them them (about one officer and twenty men), the garrison
of our first objective withholding their fire for fear of
hitting their own men. The Rifles of the captured party
had become clogged with mud and they had been lying under
heavy fire all day. A few survivors regained ROACH TRENCH
after dark. Close to the Sunken Road on our right, the
right of the right Company advanced in touch with the
8th Lincolnshire Regt., passed the second objective with
with its flank in the air and nearly reached t-he final
objective. They were however, forced to retire later
by heavy enemy bombing attacks and eventually reached
ROACH & COD TRENCHES, the latter on the extreme right.

One Officer and 25 men of the 4th Midlesex Regt.
were moved in the afternoon to reinforce Captain PEARD.
They reached him One Officer and fifteen men strong and
helped him to hold the HOOK TRENCH.

One Company of the 4th Middlesex Regt. was moved
forward from COD TRENCH to hold continuation of ROACH
TRENCH to the left, and here, drove back an enemy bombing
attack which was developing from the western edge of
ROSSIGNAL WOOD.

Lt.Col.
8th (S) Bn Somerset Light Infantry.

## PART 1 Contd.

One Company of the 13th K.R.R.C. was moved up in the afternoon to continue our Old Front Line to the left, and was afterwards ordered to withdraw into Support of the 4th Middlesex Company which covered ROSSIGNAL WOOD.

The position at the end of the day was much the same as the beginning except that we held a greater extent of ROACH TRENCH and had a post in FISH ALLEY.

A report centre was established under LT.H.K. AUSTIN approximately at K.11.b.95.25. from which much valuable information was received during the day.

Second Lieutenant H.G.STONE, Battalion Signalling Officer and one Signaller moved forward in rear of the second wave on the right, and Corporal Strawbridge on the left, running out telephone cable as they advanced. Several messages were received from these two sources during the morning until 2nd Lieut STONE was killed and Corporal Strawbridge's wire cut.

### 6.4.18.

Letter to the Battalion from Brigadier General E.L.CHALLONER C.M.G.,D.S.O. Commanding 63rd Infantry Brigade.

"I wish to thank all ranks for their splendid work and devotion to duty yesterday. The Army, Corps and Divisional Commanders also appreciate the good work and hard fighting done by the Brigade under very trying conditions yesterday and have sent their congratulations.

"I deeply regret the losses in Officers and other ranks in your Battalion, but it must be a great consolation to you to know that in addition to taking 200 prisoners, very heavy casualties were inflicted on the enemy. The Australians and New Zealanders also took heavy toll of the enemy.

"I shall be unable to speak to Units on Parade, and I shall be obliged if Commanding Officers will let the men know how very much I admire and appreciate their gallantry and good work yesterday".

### 7.4.18.

The Battalion moved back in reserve in Dugouts at E.29,a. being relieved from the Front Line by the 13th K.R.R.C. During this tour the Battalion had the following Officer casualties:-

| | |
|---|---|
| Capt H.G.BAKER | "Killed" |
| 2/Lt. H.A.DRAKEFORD. | "Killed" |
| 2/Lt. J.P.HEWITT | "Killed" |
| 2/Lt. G.H.HEARDER. | "Wounded" |
| 2/Lt. F.J.PICKARD | "Wounded" |
| 2/Lt. H.G.STONE | "Killed" |
| 2/Lt. P.J.JONES | "Missing" believed Prisoner of War. |
| 2/Lt. S.T.DYTE. | -do- |
| 2/Lt. W.E.HAYES. | -do- |
| Lt. V.L.PLANT | "Wounded" & "Missing". |

Lt.Col.
Comdg. 8th (S) Bn Somerset Light Infantry.

## PART 1 Contd.

**9.4.18.**

The Battalion moved up into Support at E.30.b.55. relieving the 15th Royal Fusiliers.

**12.4.18.**

The Battalion up into the Front Line K.6.d.7.3. relieving the 13th K.R.R.C.

**15.4.18.**

The Battalion was relieved from the Front Line by the 10th Bn Manchester Regt. On completion of relief the Battalion marched to HENU where they were billeted for One night.

**16.4.18.**

The Battalion marched into Camp (Tents) at AUTHIE (I.17.c.). Training was carried out here.

**22.4.18.**

The Battalion moved up into the Front Line at BUCQUOY (F.26.Central) relieving the 4th Bn K.O.Y.L.I.


LT.Col.
8th (S) Bn Somerset Light Infantry.

## PART 11

**28.3.18.**

Captain S.S.JENKYNS (6th Rifle Brigade attd 9th North Staffs Regt) Appointed Acting Second in Command from 28.3.18. 8th (S) Bn Somerset Light Infantry. (Authority, M.S.37836 d/-28.3.18.)

**7.4.18.**

The following Officers joined the Battalion.
CAPTAIN F.AYRES.
LIEUT. O.BRIGGS.

**12.4.18.**

HONOUR & AWARD.
The Corps Commander, under Authority deligated to him awarded the following decoration to the undernamed N.C.O.      MILITARY MEDAL
No.30207 Sergeant Anderson J.A.  8th Somerset L.I.
For conspicuous gallantry and initiative
East of YPRES 21.3.18.

**10.4.18.**

One hundred & twenty one (121) Other ranks joined the Battalion.

**19.4.18**

Ninety four (94) Other ranks joined the Battn.

**11.4.18.**

Sixty four Other Ranks joined the Battalion.

**16.4.18.**

The following Officers joined the Battalion.
LT.D.J.L.ROUTH         2/LT.F.M.J.COOK.
2/LT.D.W.WILLATT       2/LT.C.Y.FAUX.
2/LT.S.FRANKCOM.

**20.4.18.**

Six Other Ranks joined the Battalion.

**25.4.18.**

The following Oficers joined the Battalion.
CAPT.B.HOLT            2/LT.R.ERSKINE.
2/LT.W.A.G.SNELGROVE   2/LT.A.P.MASON.
2/LT.G.JACKLIN.        2/LT.W.E.BYWATER.
2/LT.A.C.SCHURIG.

Twenty four Other Ranks joined the Battalion.

Lt.Col.
Comdg. 8th (S) Bn Somerset Light Infantry.

PART 11 Contd.

**11.4.18.**
Captain (Actg Lt.Col) S.S.JENKYNS took over command of 8th (S) Bn Somerset Light Infantry. 11.4.18.

**17.4.18.**
The following Officer was invalided to England (Sick).
2/LT.J.LOCKE.
(Authority List No.1108 d/-23.4.18 O.C.1/R.R.C.H.)

TOTAL CASUALTIES FOR THE MONTH OF APRIL.

| Officers | | Other Ranks | |
|---|---|---|---|
| Killed. | 3 | Killed. | 13 |
| Wounded | 5 | Wounded | 85 |
| Missing | 3 | Missing | 84 |
| Total | 11. | Total | 182. |

**18.4.18.**
The following Officers joined the Battalion.
2/LT.C.RIGBY            (10th Royal Fusiliers)
2/LT.H.N.EYRES         (10th K.R.R.C.)
2/ LT.E.L.YARKER.     (10th Royal Fusiliers)

**26.4.18.** The following Officer was "Wounded"

2/LT.E.L.YARKER.              (10th Royal Fusiliers)

\*\*\*\*\*\*\*\*\*\*\*\*\*\*\*\*\*

Lt.Col.
8th (S) Bn Somerset Light Infantry.

63rd Brigade.
37th Division.

8th BATTALION

THE SOMERSET LIGHT INFANTRY.

MAY 1918

# WAR DIARY or INTELLIGENCE SUMMARY.

## PART 1
### WAR DIARY
### for
### MAY 1918.

**1.5.18.**
The Battalion moved back to SOUASTRE being relieved from the Front Line by 1st Battalion of the Essex Regt.

**5.5.18.**
The Battalion moved up into the left sub-sector of the PURPLE LINE at ESSARTS E.24.d.70.80. relieving the 8th Lincolnshire Regt.

**9.5.18.**
The Battalion moved up into the left sub-sector of the FRONT LINE at E.21.d.05.60. relieving the 13th K.R.R.C.

**13.5.18.**
The Battalion moved back into reserve at F.20 being relieved from the Front Line by the 4th Bn. Middlesex Regt.

**16.5.18.**
The Battalion moved back to ST. LEGER (I.12.) being relieved from the Front Line by 5th Duke of Wellington West Riding Regt. Training was carried out here.

**24.5.18.**
The Battalion moved up into the PURPLE LINE (taking over from K.19.Central to K.3.d.0.0.) relieving the 1st Canterbury Battalion of the 2nd Brigade of New Zealanders.

**30.5.18.**
The Battalion moved back into Camp at I.16.a. and I.16.c. being relieved from the Purple Line (SAILLY-au-BOIS) by the 13th Bn. Rifle Brigade.

## PART II

**7.5.18.**
One Other Rank "Wounded" (Gas).

**1.5.18.**
Three Other Ranks were "Killed" in Action.

**3.5.18.**
Eleven Other Ranks joined the Battalion.

### HONOURS & AWARDS
The Corps Commander, under Authority delegated to him, awarded the following Decoration to the undernamed:-

**MILITARY MEDAL**
No.27772 Pte LOCKYER H.J. )
No.39100 Pte GIBSON L. ) 8th Somerset L.I.

Lt. Colonel.
Commanding 8th (S) Bn Somerset Light Infantry.

## PART 11 Contd.

**4.5.18.** Forty Five (45) Other Ranks joined the Battalion.

One Other Rank "Killed in Action".

**7.5.18.** One Other Rank "Wounded in Action".

**9.5.18.** One Other Rank granted One Months leave to the United Kingdom. (Authy 1V Corps No.A.71/52 d/- 5.5.18.)

**8.5.18.** Twenty Five (25) Other Ranks joined the Battn.

Two Other Ranks were "Killed" in Action.
One Other Rank was "Wounded" in Action.

**10.5.18.** HONOURS & AWARDS
The Corps Commander, under authority delegated to him, awarded the following decoration to the undernamed:-

### MILITARY MEDAL

No.11633 Pte J.H.Rowles  )
No.38194 Pte H.R.Mullis  )
No.15448 Sgt Lambley T.  )
No.18804 Cpl Strawbridge )
No.29087 Pte F.Cousins   ) 8th Somerset L.I.
No.17091 Cpl Chapman A.H.)
No.19107 Pte J.Biggs     )
No.28424 Pte C.F.Johnson )
No.30217 Pte H.G.Green.  )

For conspicuous gallantry and
Devotion to Duty East of GOMMECOURT 5.4.18.

Capt.H.K.E.OSTLE M.C. 28th Bn London Regt. (Attd 10th Bn.York & Lancaster Regt.) to be 2nd in Command and to be Temporary Major to fill establishment 14.3.18. (Authy.Extract List 183 d/- 14.3.18.)

**8.5.18.** Thirteen (13) Other Ranks "Wounded in Action".

**7.5.18.** Five (5) Other Ranks "Wounded in Action"

**11.5.18.** Three (3) Other Ranks "Wounded in Action"

One Other Rank "Wounded" accidentally.

One Other Rank "Killed in Action"

Lt.Colonel.
Comdg. 8th (S) Bn Somerset Light Infantry.

## PART 11 Contd.

**10.5.18.** LONDON GAZETTE
Extract from London Gazette (The Times 10.5.18)
8th Somerset Light Infantry.
Lt.H.O.PRING to be Temp.Captain (Sept.21st 1917)

The following Temp. 2nd Lieuts. from York & Lancs
Regt. to be Temp. 2nd Lieuts 8th Somerset Light Infantry
with seniority specified against their names.
2nd Lieut.K.G.WOODMANSEY Oct.25th 1916.
2nd Lieut A.E.GOAD Sept.26th 1917.

**14.5.18.**
The following N.C.O. and Man was granted leave
to the United Kingdom for the period of One month
14.5.18 to 14.6.18.
No.34199 Cpl Goodlife W.L.
No.27702 Pte Poole H.
(Authy. 1VCorps No.A.71/52 d/- 5.5.18.)

**15.5.18.**
Two Other Ranks were "Wounded in Action"

One Other Rank was granted Leave to the United
Kingdom for the period of One Month.
(Authy. 1V Corps No.A.71/52 d/- 5.5.18.)

**17.5.18.** HONOURS AND AWARDS
The Field-Marshall Commanding-in-Chief has under
authority granted him by His Majesty the King, awarded
Decorations as under:-

THE DISTINGUISHED SERVICE ORDER
CAPTAIN C.J.PHARD.

THE MILITARY CROSS
LIEUT.H.K.AUSTIN.

THE DISTINGUISHED CONDUCT MEDAL
No. 7205 Sergt.Radford G.
No. 18928 Corpl.Durman W.
No. 15686 Sergt.Keith E.
No. 7869 Corpl.Haydon W.

**17.5.18**
Five (5) Other Ranks joined the Battalion.

**16.5.18**
Seventeen (17) Other Ranks joined the Battalion.

**17.5.18.**
Five (5) Other Ranks were "Wounded in Action"

Lt.Colonel.
Commanding 8th (S) Bn Somerset Light Infantry.

PART 11 Contd.

**18.5.18**
Two Other Ranks were granted "Special Leave" to the United Kingdom.

Three (3) Other Ranks joined the Battalion.

The following Officers of the 8th Somerset L.I. were transferred to the 1st Somerset Light Infantry.
Lieut. J.A. RADFORD         2nd Lt. A.G. SCHURIG.
2nd Lt. A.P. MASON.         2nd Lt. C.V. FAUX.

**20.5.18.**
HONOUR & AWARD
The Corps Commander under authority delegated to him, awarded the following decoration to the undernamed:-
THE MILITARY MEDAL.
No. 16545 Sergt. Perkins A.       8th Somerset L.I.

Eleven (11) Other Ranks joined the Battalion.

**22.5.18.**
The following Officer was invalided to England (Sick) (Auth'y. List No. 1137 d/- 22.5.18.)
2nd Lieut. S. FRANKCOM.

**25.5.18.**
Two (2) Other Ranks were "Killed" in Action.

Two (2) Other Ranks were "Wounded" in Action.

**27.5.18.**
The following Officer joined the Battalion.
Lieut. E.C.W. ROWLEY (11th R. Warwick Regt.)

One Other Rank was "Wounded in Action"

TOTAL CASUALTIES FOR THE MONTH.

Other Ranks.

"Killed"     9
"Wounded"   36
             ---
Total       45

                                    Lt. Colonel.
Commanding 8th (S) Bn Somerset Light Infantry.

63rd Brigade.
37th Division.

8th BATTALION

THE SOMERSET LIGHT INFANTRY

JUNE 1918

## PART 1

# WAR DIARY

## --for--
## JUNE. 1918.
*********************

**5.6.18.**
The Battalion moved by Busses to Billets at PICQUIGNY.
Embussed at I.15.a.3.9. about 1 a.m.
Debussed at PICQUIGNY about 7 a.m.
During our stay here Training was carried out.

**10.6.18.**
The Battalion moved by Busses from PICQUIGNY to the CONTY Area.
Embussed at PICQUIGNY about 11 a.m.
Debussed at NAMPTY about 4 p.m.
The same day the Battalion marched into Billets at PROUZEL.
Left NAMPTY about 9 p.m. and arrived at PROUZEL about 10.30 p.m.
Training was carried out here.

**12.6.18.**
The Battalion marched into Billets at ST.SAUFLIEU.
Left PROUZEL about 9.30 p.m. and arrived at ST.SAUFLIEU about 11 p.m.
Training was carried out here.

**19.6.18.**
The Battalion Marched to Billets at PROUZEL.
Left ST.SAUFLIEU about 11 p.m. and arrived at PROUZEL about 12.30 a.m.

**21.6.18.**
The Battalion moved by Rail from PROUZEL to MONDICOURT.
Entrained at PROUZEL about 8.35 a.m. and arrived at MONDICOURT about 2.p.m.
The Battalion then marched to Camp (Canvas) at COUIN. Training was carried out here.

**25.6.18.**
The Battalion moved up into the Left Sub-Sector of the Front Line with Headquarters at F.21.c.4.6. relieving the 5th K.O.Y.L.I.
Rear Bn.Hd.Qrs at SOUASTRE.

.......................Capt. for Lt.Colonel.
Commanding 8th (S) Bn Somerset Light Infantry.

## PART 11

**23.5.18.**

### MENTIONED IN DESPATCHES

LIEUT. H. PIKE. 8th Som.L.I.
No.14764 Sgt. F. PARSONS. 8th Som.L.I.

**25.5.18.**

2nd Lt. R.H. BUTTON invalided to England and struck off the strength.
(Authy. List No.1145 d/- 30.5.18 (2/B.R.C.H.)

**31.5.18.**

35 (Thirty five) Other Ranks joined the Battalion.
One Other Rank granted Special Leave to the United Kingdom from 31.5.18 to 7.6.18.

**1.6.18.**

One Other Rank proceeded to England as Candidate for Temporary Commission.

**2.6.18.**

2nd Lt. H.G. WARD joined the Battalion.

**3.6.18.**

13 Other Ranks joined the Battalion.

**3.6.18.**

The King has been pleased, on the occasion of His Majesty's Birthday, to award the following decoration to the under-mentioned for valuable services rendered in connection with Military Operations in the Field.

### DISTINGUISHED SERVICE MEDAL

No.15173 Sgt A. ISAACS. 8th Som.L.I.

**4.6.18.**

3 (Three) Other Ranks joined the Battalion.

**5.6.18.**

Capt.(a/Lt.Col.) S.S. JENKYNS relinquished the Command of this Battalion, and appointed Corps Educational Officer.

**6.6.18.**

Temp. Major (a/Lt.Col.) J.H.M. HARDYMAN. M.C. took over Command of the Battalion.

**9.6.18.**

The Field Marshal Commanding-in-chief, under authority granted to him by His Majesty the King awarded the following decoration to the undernamed Officer for gallantry in the Field.

### MILITARY CROSS

2/Lt. A.C. OWEN.    8th Somerset L.I.

.................... Capt. for Lt. Colonel
Commanding 8th (S) Bn Somerset Light Infantry.

Army Form C. 2118.

PART 11 Contd.
***********

**11.6.18.** The Field Marshal Commanding-in-Chief under Authority granted to him by His Majesty the King, made the following award to the undermentioned for gallantry in the Field during recent operations.

MILITARY MEDAL.

No.18854 L/c TAYLOR G.  8th Somerset L.I.

---

One Other Rank proceeded to England as Candidate for Temporary Commission.

**16.6.18.** 2 (Two) Other Ranks joined the Battalion.

**17.6.18.** LIEUT D.H.COX proceeded to England for attachment to the Machine Gun Training Centre GRANTHAM. (Authy.No.A/D 111/127 d/-11th June 1918)

**23.6.18.** One Other Rank proceeded to England as Candidate for Temporary Commission.

**24.6.18.** His Majesty has been pleased to approve of the following awards for valuable services rendered in the Field.

MERITORIOUS SERVICE MEDAL

No.30841 R.S.M. J.HANLEY.  8th Somerset L.I.
No.15517 Sergt.WALTERS E.  8th Somerset L.I.

TOTAL CASUALTIES FOR THE MONTH.

3 (Three) Other Ranks.  "Wounded"

*L.J.Peard.*
...........Capt. for Lt.Col.
Commanding 8th(S) Bn Somerset Light Infantry.

63rd Brigade,
37th Division.

8th BATTALION

THE SOMERSET LIGHT INFANTRY

JULY 1918

PART 1

## WAR DIARY for JULY 1918.

**6.7.18.** On the night of 7th/8th July the Battalion was relieved from the FRONT LINE by the 13th Bn. K.R.R.C., and on completion of the relief moved back to the VALLEY CAMP at SOUASTRE.

**10.7.18.** On the night of 10th/11th July the Battalion evacuated VALLEY CAMP.
Our "B" Company relieved "D" Company of the 8th Lincolnshire Regt in the CHATEAU DE LA HAYE SWITCH LINE with Company Headquarters at E.19.a.8.7.
The remainder of the Battalion moved into Billets at SOUASTRE.

**11.7.18.** On night of 11th/12th July "A" Company of this Battalion joined "B" Company in the CHATEAU DE LA HAYE SWITCH LINE.

**12.7.18.** On night of 13th/14th July the Battalion relieved the 1st Bn. Essex Regt. in SUPPORT at E.30.a.10.55.

**17.7.18.** On night of 17th/18th July the Battalion moved up into the FRONT LINE (Left sector of the Brigade Front) relieving the 8th Bn Lincoln. Regt.

**25.7.18.** On night of 26th/27th July the Battalion was relieved from the FRONT LINE by the 10th Bn. Royal Fusiliers and took over from the 13th Rifle Brigade with Battalion Headquarters at E.23.c.60.00.

**29.7.18.** On the night of 29th/30th July the Battalion moved back to the VALLEY CAMP at SOUASTRE being relieved by the 8th Bn. Lincolnshire Regt.

Lt. Colonel.
Commanding 8th (S) Bn Somerset Light Infantry.

## PART 11

**8.7.18.** 2nd Lt.C.C.R. PALMER, 2nd Lt.L.N.FORD and 16 Other Ranks joined the Battalion.

**9.7.18.** 2nd Lt.G.JACKLIN proceeded to England for employment with the Royal Air Force. (Authy.A.G.2154/276 (O)) dated 25.6.18)

The following Officers joined the Battalion.
2nd Lt.W.J.SCOTT.
2nd Lt.H.STONE.

**10.7.18.** 2nd Lt. R.T.J.TRENT joined the Battalion.

**11.7.18.** 2nd Lt.S.G.STEARS joined the Battalion.

**14.7.18.** Extract from List No.195 d/- 7.7.18 Appointments, Commissions &c, approved by the Field Marshall Commanding-in-Chief.
8th (S) Bn Somerset Light Infantry.
Temp.Capt.H. O.PRING to be ADJUTANT vice Temp.Capt.P.C.HAGON. 28th Dec. 1918.

**15.7.18.** One other rank granted Special Leave to the United Kingdom. Period 15.7.18 to 29.7.18.

**17.7.18.** One Other Rank granted One Months (Re-engegement) leave to the United Kingdom. Period. 17.7.18 to 17.8.18.

**16.7.18.** Fourty-four (44) Other Ranks joined the Battalion.

**20.7.18.** Three Other Ranks were granted leave to the United Kingdom. Period 20.7.18 to 3.8.18.

Capt. F. AYRES proceeded to England for employment with the Royal Air Force. (Authy.A.G.2154/276 (O)25.6.18)

One N.C.O. proceeded to England as Candidate for Temp. Commission.

One Other Rank proceeded to England on Re-engagement (One month) from 20.7.18 to 20.8.18.

Lt.Colonel.
Commanding 8th ( S) Bn Somerset Light Infantry.

PART 11 Contd.

**23.7.18.** One Other granted leave to the United Kingdom. Period 23.7.18 to 4.8.18.

Three Other Ranks granted leave to the United Kingdom. Period 23.7.18 to 6.8.18.

**24.7.18.** Capt. E. C. Cartwright joined the Battalion.

**25.7.18.** 2nd Lt. C.G. Miles joined the Battalion.

Lt. H.PIKE pr oceeded to England on Six months Tour of Duty.
(Authy.A.G.2158/4392 (O))

**28.7.18.** 2nd Lt. (a/ Capt) H.K.POPLE proceeded to England for employment with the Royal Air Force. (Authy. A.G.2154/301 (O)).

**29.7.18.** One Other rank granted leave to the United Kingdom. Period. 29.7.18. to 12.8.18.

Two N.C.O's granted leave in FRANCE (ST.VALERY) from 29.7.18 to 5.8.18.

**13.7.18.** 2nd Lt. W. D. WILLATT invalided to England (Sick)
(Authy.Base Order No.50 d/- 13.7.18.

TOTAL CASUALTIES FOR MONTH.
\*\*\*\*\*\*\*\*\*\*\*\*\*\*\*\*\*\*\*\*\*\*\*\*\*\*

Other Ranks.

"Wounded at Duty". 2
"Wounded" 25
"Killed" 7
-----
34
-----

Lt.Colonel.
Commanding 8th (S) Bn Somerset Light Infantry.

63rd Brigade.
37th Division.

8th BATTALION

THE SOMERSET LIGHT INFANTRY

AUGUST 1918

PART I.

WAR DIARY

for

August. 1918.

**5.8.18.**
On the night of 5th/6th. the battalion moved up into the front line relieving the 4th Batt Middlesex Regt.
Battalion Headquarters at F.21.c.40.70.

**11.8.18.**
On the night of 10th/11th August the enemy attempted a raid.
(See Map Sheet 57d. N.E. 1/20000 )
At about 3-10 a.m. the enemy opened an intense bombardment of artillery and trench mortars on our post line which ran approximately F.22.b.50.00 - F.20.c.50.30.- L.3.b.25.60. and also on the support trench (DURHAM TRENCH) F.27.b.75.50 - F.26.b.85.00.
The barrage put down on the front line posts was a creeping one and under cover of this the enemy advanced along the railway running east and west in F.22.b.
The garrisons put up a stubborn resistance at their posts F.26.d.15.80 and F.26.1.30.90- F.26.b.50.00.
It was quite dark at the time and the enemy being in considerable strength (about 60) succeeded in driving through out positions at F.26.d.15.80.and F.22.b.50.00.
The garrisons of these posts retired to a defensive position about F.22.b.9.2.
From this position Private Osborne organised a counter attack which was completely successful, driving the enemy out of the posts which he had captured and causing him to retire to his normal line.
As the enemy retired he was caught very successfully in our S.O.S. barrage which inflicted many casualties and caused entire confusion. Whistling and shouting could be heard in all directions.
It is evident that the enemy had definitely intended no only to capture the garrisons of the posts but to occupy the posts themselves, for in the haversacks which were found next day were two bottles of water and two days' rations.
One of the outstanding incidents of this raid was the fact that immediately the S.O.S. signal was sent up Lt-Col F.H.W.Hardyman ..... D.S.O. who was then commanding the Battalion at once rushed off to the scene of action and his presence probably made a great difference to the moral of the men concerned, for they were only boys, who had seen little or no previous service.

Geo.W.Sheringham
Lt.Col.
Commanding 8th (S) Bn. Somerset Light Infantry

Page 2.

## PART II. (Contd)

**12. 8.18.**

The enemy attempted another raid.

At about 4 a.m. on the morning of the 12th a party of the enemy, about 15 strong were seen approaching our post at L.3.b.7.8.

They attacked with bombs under cover of heavy machine gun fire, but our bombing, Lewis Gun and rifle fire drove them off successfully.

Next morning when the ground was examined it was found that the wire in front of this post had been cut in five places and also that each man of the attacking party had taken up a defensive position for himself behind a tree, indicated ~~as was pointed out~~ by the fact that a little heap of empty cartridge cases was to be found behind each tree of any size in the immediate neighbourhood.

**17.8.18.**

The battalion moved back to FONQUEVILLERS being relieved by 13th Rifle Brigade and taking over billets from the 9th North Staffs Regt.

**19.8.18.**

The battalion moved up into the front line relieving the 1st Battn. Essex Regt.

Operations for period 21st to 26th August 1918 see seperate report.

**26.8.18.**

The Battalion moved back to ACHIET-le-PETIT on the morning of 26th inst and occupied derelict huts at MXXXXX. G.14.a.( 57C. N.W.)

The undermentioned Officers, N.C.O's and men of the 8th Somerset Light Infantry did exceptionally good work during the operations carried out between 21st to 26th August 1918.

CAPT. G.SIMS. M.C.  2/Lt.(a/Capt) C.H.MADDEN.
2/Lt.R.ERSKINE.  2/Lt.H.M.EYRE S.
CAPT.B.HOLT.

No.7725 C.S.M.Yaw. R. No.21436 L/c Marley J.
No.30063 Cpl Holder W. No.30501 Pte Pagington. E.
No.36663 Pte Williams A. No.28432 Pte Lindsay J.W.

Lt Colonel.
Commanding 8th (S) Bn.Somerset Light Infantry.

# WAR DIARY or INTELLIGENCE SUMMARY

PART 11

| Place | Date | Hour | Summary of Events and Information | Remarks and references to Appendices |
|---|---|---|---|---|
| | 5.8.18. | | Fourty Six (46) Other ranks joined the Battalion. | |
| | 6.8.18. | | The following extract from List No.198 dated 28.7.18. Appointments, Commissions Etc. approved by the Field Marshal Commanding-in-Chief. 8th (S) Bn Somerset Light Infantry. CAPT. C.J.PEARD D.S.O. (SR) to be Acting Major whilst employed as 2nd -in-Command. | |
| | 8.8.18. | | 2nd Lt.C.McLEOD joined the Battalion and taken on the strength from 29.7.18. | |
| | 6..8.18. | | LIEUT. A.C.OWEN M.C. "Killed in Action". | |
| | 9.8.18. | | One Other Rank granted leave to U/K. from 9.8.18 to 23.8.18. | |
| | 11.8.18. | | Major C.J.PEARD D.S.O. and Eight Other Ranks granted leave to U/K from 11.8.18 to 25.8.18. | |
| | 13.8.18. | | Five Other Ranks joined the Battalion. | |
| | 15.8.18. | | Five Other Ranks granted Leave to U/K from 15.8.18 to 29.8.18. | |
| | 12.8.18. | | One Other Rank granted leave to PARIS from 12.8.18 to 21.8.18. | |
| | 10.8.18. | | LIEUT K.G.WOODMANSEY granted leave to U/K from 10.8.18 to 24.8.18. | |
| | 12.8.18. | | Two Other Ranks joined the Battalion. | |
| | 11.8.18 | | Three Other Ranks joined the Battalion. | |
| | 15.8.18. | | Lt.E.C.V.ROWLEY M.C. proceeded to England for employment on probation with the R.A.F. (Authy.A.G.2154/316 (O)) R.S.M.J.HANLEY proceeded to join 1st Bn. Royal Warwickshire Regt. as Quartermaster. (Authy.A.G.2158/4980 (O)) | |
| | 18.8.18. | | Thirty two (32) Other Ranks joined the Battalion. | |
| | 17.8.18. | | Lieut.O.BRIGGS granted leave to U/K from 17.8.18 to 31.8.18. | |
| | 18.8.18. | | Lieut. P.H.R.BENNETT and Eight Other Ranks granted leave to U/K from 18.8.18 to 1.9.18. | |

Lt. Colonel.
Commanding 8th (S) Bn Somerset Light Infantry.

## PART 11 Contd.

**22.8.18.** Five Other Ranks granted leave to U/K from 22.8.18 to 4.9.18.

**19.8.18.** One N.C.O. proceeded to England as Candidate for Temp. Commission.

**23.8.18.** 2/Lt. R.A.FORREST transferred to 63rd Brigade Headquarters as Intelligence Officer. (Authy. G.R.O. 4763.)

Nineteen (19) Other Ranks joined the Battalion.

**18.8.18.** 2nd Lt. R.HENDERSON joined the Battn.

**26.8.18.** The following Officers joined the Battn.
2/Lt.J.H.LUGG.      2/Lt.L.P.B.DOMAN.
2/Lt. D.A.MACKAY.

**24.8.18.** LIEUT. J.H.M.HARDYMAN D.S.O..M.C. was "Killed in Action".

2/Lt.W.A.G.SHELGROVE and 2/Lt.H.M.EYRES were "Wounded in Action".

**23.8.18.** Lt.(a/Capt) C.H.SIMS M.C. and 2/Lt. R. ERSKINE were "Wounded in Action".

**24.8.18.** Major J.G.BOSS took over the Command of the Battalion.

**29.8.18.** Five Other Ranks granted leave to U/K from 29.8.18 to 11.9.18.

**27.8.18.** The undernamed were awarded the following decoration.
MILITARY MEDAL.
No.207828 Sgt E.Cope.         )
No. 27662 L/c E.Millard.      ) 8th Somerset L.I.
No. 28778 Pte T.Lewis.        )
No. 28467 Pte G.Smart.        )
For conspicuous gallantry and devotion to duty at BUCQUOY.

**30.8.18.** LT.COLONEL C.J.de B.SHERINGHAM M.C. took over Command of the Battalion. vice Lt.Col. BOSS to 8th Bn Lincolnshire Regt.

**31.8.18.** The undernamed Officers joined the Battn.
2/Lt.G.H.ROOD.
2/Lt.E.J.K.GRIMES.
2/Lt.F.LEVY.
2/Lt.G.H.MATTHEWS.
2/Lt.H.W.BROOKS.

Lt.Colonel.
Commanding 8th (S) Bn Somerset Light Infantry.

## PART 11 Contd.

**26.8.18.**
2/Lt. C.C.R. PALMER "Wounded in Action".

**25.8.18.**
Capt. B. HOLT and Eight Other Ranks granted Leave to U/K from 25.8.18 to 7.9.18.

TOTAL CASUALTIES FOR THE MONTH.

| | |
|---|---|
| Officers Killed. | 2 |
| Officers Wounded. | 6 |
| Other Ranks Killed. | 21 |
| Other Ranks Wounded. | 111 |
| Missing. | 12 |

Lt;Colonel.
Commanding 8th (S) Bn Somerset Light Infantry.

REPORT ON OPERATIONS CARRIED OUT BY

8th (S) Bn. Somerset Light Infantry.
21st to 26th August 1918.
================================================

(See Map, Sheet 57d N.E. 1/20,000 )
The Battalion came into the line in and West of BUCQUOY
on night of 19th/20th August 1918.
    The Objective to be reached was the enemy's main line
of resistance L.4.a.93.54. to T.29.d.45.90 which lay about
300 yards on the reverse side of the high ground East of
BUCQUOY. The battalion was organised with two companies in
the Front Line of the attack and two companies in support.
    Battalion Headquarters was about 300 yards West of
BUCQUOY and a Battle Headquarters was to be established
in BUCQUOY CEMETERY ( held by the enemy before the attack).
    ZERO hour was 4-50 a.m. at which time it was fairly
light, but there was a very heavy mist which prevented
visibility of more than about 40 yards.
    The Artillery barrage was remarkably good and accurate
and greatly assisted our infantry in their work.
    The Battalion advanced straight to its objective
with very few casualties and quickly got in touch with the
units on each flank;
    About 60 prisoners and 6 machine guns were captured.
    Our Battle Headquarters was established at the S.E.
tip of the Cemetery immediately the barrage had cleared from
it.
    Tanks co-operated very successfully.
    As soon as the objective was gained the battalion
was organised in depth- two companies in the front line and
two companies in support.

(See Map Sheet 57c N.W. )
    The 5th Division passed over the battalion about
¾ of an hour after the objective had been taken, and advanced,
taking ACHIET-le-PETIT and LOGEAST WOOD.
    This battalion remained in the defensive positions
on the high ground East of BUCQUOY during the following night
and day.
    On the night of 22nd/23rd the battalion moved into
reserve assembly positions East of ABLAINZEVILLE.
    The following morning at 11-30 a.m. two companies of
of the battalion provided mopping up parties to work with
the tanks during the attack on ACHIET-le-GRAND.
This mopping up party captured about 500 prisoners and
15 Machine Guns.
    At 6 p.m. orders were received for the battalion to
take over the line in front of BIHUCOURT and at about 8-30 p.m.
they had moved up to do so, but it was found that an enemy
machine gun pocket still remained just south of BIHUCOURT.
    During the night 23rd/24th one company attacked this
pocket and half occupied it, thus practically ensuring the
safety of the right flank of BIHUCOURT which had previously
been in the air.

On the morning of 24th the New Zealand Division attacked and captured GREVILLERS and the 63rd Brigade was to co-operate and form a defensive flank on the left.

The Battalion moved off at Zero and captured its objective in BIEFVILLERS, but owing to the fact that the left flank was in the air and the village was extremely heavily bombarded it was evacuated and a position taken up on the high ground immediately West.

It was during a personal reconnaissance of this position that the Commanding Officer Lieut-Colonel J.H.M.HARDYMAN M.C. was killed by a shell.

He had previously moved up with his battalion headquarters to this position in a tank.

During the advance on BIEFCOURT 3 5"9 Howitzers were captured also 15 prisoners and 3 Machine guns.

At 5 a.m. on 25th the Battalion moved in support to the Brigade and captured the quarry North of BIHUCOURT and hung onto it while the remainder of the Brigade established posts in front. During this operation about 30 prisoners and 4 machine guns were captured.

That evening the Brigade was in reserve to the successful attack on FAVREUIL and at about 3 a.m. the 26th was relieved by 15th Battn. Royal Warwickshire Regt. during a very heavy bombardment.

The total casualties during the operation were:-

Officers Killed.       1.
"        Wounded.      5.

Other Ranks. Killed.   31.
"    "    Wounded.    119.
"    "    Missing      9.
"    "    I. Gas.     13.
"    "    Missing
         believed Killed.  6.

Captured.

Prisoners     300
Trench Mortars.  2.
Machine Guns.   14.
S.S Hows.        3.

-----------------------------------

Lt Col.
Commanding 8th (S) Bn. Somerset Light Infantry.

63rd Brigade.
37th Division.

8th BATTALION

THE SOMERSET LIGHT INFANTRY

SEPTEMBER 1ST 1918

PART II

| | |
|---|---|
| Place | |
| Date | |
| Hour | |

1.9.18. The Field Marshal-Commanding-in-Chief under authority granted by His Majesty the KING awarded the following Decorations:-

THE DISTINGUISHED SERVICE ORDER.
------------------------------------
T/Lt.Colonel J.H.M.Hardyman M.C.

THE MILITARY CROSS.
-------------------
2/Lieut. R.T.J.Trent.

THE DISTINGUISHED CONDUCT MEDAL.
--------------------------------
No.19140 Private T.Osborne.

31.8.18. 110 Other Ranks joined the Battalion.

1.9.18. 2/Lt.L.C.Bodey and 8 (eight) Other Ranks granted 14 days leave to U/K.

2/Lt.J.Morton joined the Battalion.

6.9.18. Capt W.J.Bennett and Lieut K.C.Woodmansey "Wounded" in Action.

5.9.18. 5 (five) Other Ranks granted 14 days leave to U/K.

9.9.18 8 (eight) Other Ranks granted 14 days leave to U/K.

8.9.18. 2/Lt.C.C.Miles invalided (Sick) to England.

7.9.18. 2/Lt.C.Matthews "Wounded in Action".

9.9.18. 12 (twelve) Other Ranks joined the Battalion.

11.9.18. 5 (five) Other Ranks granted 14 days leave to U/K.

12.9.18. 1 (One) Other Ranks granted leave (14 days) to U/K.

*C.B.Sheringham*
Lt.Colonel.
Commanding 8th (S) Bn Somerset Light Infantry.

**WAR DIARY or INTELLIGENCE SUMMARY**

Army Form C. 2118.

| Hour, Date, Place | Summary of Events and Information |
|---|---|
| 9.8.18. | The Band of the 8th (S) Bn Somerset Light Infantry played for His Majesty the KING at FORT MAHON. |
| 13.9.18. | The Corps Commander under authority granted by His Majesty the KING awarded the following decorations to the undernamed for "Conspicuous gallantry and devotion to duty during the operations from August 21st to 26th 1918.

THE MILITARY MEDAL.

No.15707 Sgt Peavley W.
No.21436 L/c Marley J.
No.40055 Pte Edwards V.
No.27358 Pte Bough H.
No.15379 Cpl Redford E.
No.29786 Pte Gillett W.
No.28346 Pte Baker H. |
| 12.9.18. | 12 (twelve) Other Ranks joined the Battalion. |
| 14.9.18. | The following letter was received from Brigadier E.L.CHALLONER C.M.G., D.S.O. Commanding 63rd Infantry Brigade.
" I wish to thank you, your Officers, N.C.O's and men and to place on record, my appreciation of the exceptionally good work, great endurance and determination displayed by all ranks in the operations around HAVRINCOURT WOOD from 3rd Sept. to 11th Sept. 1918.
" The duties of clearing up the Wood and establishing a line east and north of it presented many difficulties owing to the nature of the ground and heavy enemy shelling. That this was done so successfully, and with such light casualties, reflects the greatest credit on all ranks.
" Your Battalion has again, therefore, added to it's already long list of honours and I feel sure will continue to do so with the same gallantry and devotion to the end which is now in sight." |
| 16.9.18. | The following Officers and 8 (eight) Other Ranks were granted 14 days Leave to U/K.
Capt. C.H.MADDEN M.C.
Lieut. H.A.WALNE. M.C.
Lieut. H.K.AUSTIN M.C. |

**Remarks and references to Appendices**

| | |
|---|---|
| 10.9.18. | 2/Lieut W.Deeming invalided (Sick) to England. |
| 18.9.18. | 4 (four) Other Ranks granted 14 days Leave to U/K. |
| 19.9.18. | 1 (One) Other Rank granted 14 days leave to U/K. |
| 15.9.18. | 2/Lt.T.E.DAVEY joined the Battalion. |

*[signature]*
Lt.Colonel.
Commanding 8th (S) Bn Somerset Light Infantry.

PART 11

18.9.18.  The following Officers became casualties in action.
          2/Lt.C.McLEOD.        "Wounded"
          2/Lt.G.H.ROOD.         "
          2/Lt.F.LEVY           "Injured Gas"

19.9.18.  2/Lt.C.C.R.PALMER joined the Battalion.

21.9.18.  1 (one) Other Ranks granted "Special Leave to the U/K for 14 days.

23.9.18.  11 (eleven) Other Ranks granted leave (14 days) to U/K.

22.9.18.  The Field Marshal Commanding-in-Chief under authority granted to him by His Majesty the KING awarded decorations as under to the following for
          "Conspicuous gallantry and devotion to duty East of BUCQUOY during operations 21st to 26th August 1918."

          BAR TO THE MILITARY CROSS.
            Capt. G.H.SIMS M.C.

          The MILITARY CROSS.
            Capt. B.HOLT.
            Capt. C.H.MADDEN.

          THE DISTINGUISHED CONDUCT MEDAL.
            No. 7725 C.S.M.Yaw R.
            No.36663 Pte A.Williams.
            No.30501 Pte Paginton E.

12.9.18.  2/Lt.R.T.J.TRENT M.C. invalided (Sick) to England.

23.9.18.  12 (twelve) Other Ranks joined the Battalion.
          One N.C.O. proceeded to England as Candidate for Temporary Commission.

26.9.18.  Lieut & Qr.Mr. D.G.CAMPBELL granted leave (14 days) to U/K.
          One N.C.O. granted 14 days leave to U/K.

25.9.18.  5 (five) Other Ranks joined the Battalion.

11.9.18.  Lieut V.G.WILLATT invalided (Sick) to England.

25.9.18.  5 (five) N.C.O's despatched to England for exchange & 6 months tour of Home Duty.

                              *C.B.Kerningham*
                              Lt. Colonel
          Commanding 8th (8) Bn Somerset Light Infantry.

PART v11

**27.9.18.**  The Corps Commander under authority granted by His Majesty the King awarded the following decoration to the undernamed for "gallantry and devotion to duty near HAVRINCOURT on 8th September 1918."

THE MILITARY MEDAL.

No.202862 Cpl E.J.WILLEY.
No.28273 Pte VARNDELL F.
No.28432 Pte J.W.LINDSEY.
No.13708 Pte W.POWELL.
No. 6892 Cpl W.J.JACKSON.

**29.9.18.**  One Other Rank proceeded to England as Candidate for Temporary Commission.

**16.9.18.**  2/Lt.W.WOOD invalided (Sick) to England.

**30.9.18.**  11 Other Ranks granted 14 days leave to U/K.

One Other Ranks granted re-engagement leave for One Month, to U/K.

TOTAL CASUALTIES FOR THE MONTH.

Officers
    Wounded 5.

Other Ranks
    Killed     12
    Wounded   88
    Missing    2

*[signature]*
Lt.Colonel.
Commanding 8th (S) Bn Somerset Light Infantry.

PART 1

WAR DIARY for
September
1918

| Date | | |
|---|---|---|
| 3.9.18. | The Battalion moved up into Support relieving a Battalion of the K.O.S.B's. | |
| | For Operations - period 3rd to 11th Sept. 1918 see separate Report. | |
| 11th to 15th | See operation order No. 96 attached | |
| 16.9.18. | The 63rd Infantry Brigade relieved the 111th Infantry Brigade in the Support Line with this Battalion in the Main Line of Resistance at P.4, and P.2. | |
| 18.9.18. | The Battalion moved forward to P.12.a. and P.6.c. | |
| 20.9.18. | The Battalion moved back to LEBUCQUIERE being relieved by the 1st/5th East Lancs Regt. | |
| 21.9.18. | The Battalion moved back to a Camp at LIGNY THILLOY, where it stayed until 30.9.18. During this period training was carried out daily. | |
| 30.9.18. | The Battalion moved forward to BERTINCOURT, leaving LIGNY THILLOY at 7.15 a.m. and arriving at BERTINCOURT about 11 a.m. | |

G. de B. Sheringham
Lt. Colonel.
Commanding 8th (S) Bn Somerset Light Infantry.

REPORT ON OPERATIONS
CARRIED OUT BY
8th (S) Bn SOMERSET LIGHT INFANTRY
from 3rd to 11th Sept. 1918.
**********************************

Sept. 3.    The Battalion was in Billets at ACHIET le PETIT. Orders were received at 2.50 p.m. to move forward at once to the neighbourhood of FAVREUIL, definite orders to be issued later.
            The Battalion had previously been placed at half an hours' notice and left Camp at 3.20 p.m. in the following Order: "HQ", "D", "C", "B", & "A" Coy. Route: ACHIET le GRAND - BIHUCOURT - thence to South of SAPIGNIES by track to MONUMENT halting at H.15.d.4.4. for tea at about 5p.m.
            A start was made again at about 7 p.m. and the march continued after orders had been received re Units to be relieved. The Battalion relieved a Battalion of the K.O.S.B's in I.29 West of LEBUCQUIERE and bivouaced for the night in this area with Battalion Headquarters at I.29.d.6.2.

Sept. 4.    The following morning Companies were ordered to send out Patrols at dawn to keep in touch with the 112th Infantry Brigade and to be ready to move at a moments notice. "D" Coy on Right, "C" Coy on left, "B" Coy in Support and "A" Coy in Reserve. Patrols reported at 7.30 a.m. no troops in sight from P.3.a., so "D" Coy and "C" Coy moved to line J.32.b & c. P.2.a. with Support Coy in P.1.a. and Reserve Coy at I.36.d.8.2. On Learning from forward patrols of the situation, permission from Brigade was asked at 10.35 a.m. to move to line P.3.a. J.33. This was obtained and at 12.30 p.m. Order No.2 was issued moving forwarded the Battalion as stated.
            Battalion Headquarters moved to J.31.d.2.2. and later owing to shelling to J.32.a.5.3.
            The night and the following day were spent in this position.

Sept. 5th.  Orders were received during the morning that the Battalion was to relieve 2nd Canterbury Battalion, New Zealand Division and 1st Essex, 112th Infantry Brigade.
            Commanding Officer and Company Officers accordingly met at Headquarters 2nd Canterbury Battn. at P.9.d.65.65. Forward positions were reconnoitred and the Battalion moved up between 7 p.m. and 9 p.m. "D" Coy with its right in touch with Newzealanders on MATHESON ROAD at about P.12.a.2.5. A gap existed between the Newzealanders and the 1st Essex Regt. "D" Coy were ordered to establish a post at about P.6.c.Central and "C" Coy at P.6.c.8.7.
            "C" Coy took over from 1st Essex in Sunken Road. from P.6.d.4.8. to P.6.b.85.30.
            "B" Coy was in support about PAUPER TRENCH in P.10.b & d.
            "A" Coy in Reserve at about P.10.a.5.8.
            The above relief was completed about 1 a.m. on 7th, and was greatly impeded by the very severe shelling of RUYAULCOURT by the enemy, probably in retaliation for the New Zealand advance in the afternoon.
            In this shelling Capt.W.J.BENNETT, Officer Comdg. "B" Coy, Lt.WOODMANSEY, 2/Lt.MATTHEWS, Sgt.Cullender and several others were wounded.

An attempt was made by the enemy during the night to
surprise and cut off right post of Left Company at about
P.6.d.30.00 but failed.
            The dispositions that night were as shown on map
attached - with Battalion Headquarters at P.2.b.5.5.

Sept.6.     It had been reported that the enemy had vacated
P.24.A.30.  Patrols were pushed forward to see if
enemy had evacuated his posts West of Wood, but these
patrols were fired on from P.12b.
            Orders were sent out to push strong patrols
forward at dusk if possible to edge of Wood, unless
this could be done sooner.
            At about 5 p.m. the Right Company acting in
conjunction with New Zealand Division on their right
advanced their lines to Western edge of HAVRINCOURT
WOOD.
            The Left Company conforming but being unable
to get forward on their left so far, owing to the
necessity of throwing back their left flank.
            The front line of posts was established
along line Q.7.a.30.30 - Q.1.d.30.20 thence along
track running North easterly direction through Wood.
            "B" Coy moved up to P.12.a.5.5. and "A" Coy
moved into PANZER TRENCH P.12.b.

Sept.7.     At 2.15 a.m. on the 7th inst, the advance was
continued due east "D" Coy reaching vicinity of
PLAGUE MONUMENT - CHAFF TRENCH and Q.8.d.31.85. then
"C" Coy reached CLAYTON CROSS at 7 a.m. -
touch obtained with right Company but not with 8th
Lincolns. Defensive flank to left formed. Enemy
was located in QUADRANGLE TRENCH. From this time
onwards enemy shelling was severe, meantime, "D"
Coy pushed up two platoons to West edge of Wood in
Support to "D" Coy and two platoons further in Support
to "C" Coy.
            At about 1 p.m. word being received that the
New Zealanders were trying to get on South West of
TRESCAULT and would be assisted greatly by our
attempting a further advance. An effort was made
to reach Q.3.d.1.5. and BUHLER TRENCH, but owing to
determined enemy resistance and Machine Gun fire this
further advance was held up. Casualties were, however,
inflicted on the enemy. A post at Cross Roads Q.a.O.6.
was forced to withdraw and the line for the night was
established from Q.3.d.5.4. to Q.3.a.3.5. - QUADRANGLE
TRENCH to Q.9.a.0.4. along Road to Q.8.b.0.5. to
Q.8.c.4.7. thence to HUBERT AVENUE.
            "C" Coy having been obliged to desist from effort
to bomb east along HINDENBURG RESERVE owing to fact that
TRENCH was not continuous, and that enemy machine guns
were trained on BARNUM HILL ROAD across which bombing
bombing party would have had to pass. Casualties were
suffered at this point in endeavouring to get on. Touch
with New Zealanders on right and Lincolns on left was
maintained. In order to connect up above line it was
found necessary to put two platoons of "B" Coy into the
line along Southern side of Road running East and West
through Q.8.b.
            2/Lt.TODD rendered great assistance in putting
out this line of posts.
            The remaining two platoons of "B" Coy occupied
RUSSELL AVENUE & QUADRANGLE TRENCH South of Cross Roads
in Q.8.b.

**Sept. 8.** On the following morning patrols were pushed forward up QUADRANGLE TRENCH and TUNNEL AVENUE and found no trace of enemy. Reports being received at 4 p.m. a further advance was at once ordered and before night-fall the line SHROPSHIRE RESERVE thence through Woods, BUTLER RESERVE along TUNNEL AVENUE to Q.3.d.1.5. "A" Coy on right and "B" Coy on Left.
Touch with 8th Lincolns at Q.3.b.4.4.
Operation Order No.94 was then issued at 1 a.m. on 9th. 4th Middlesex Regt. relieved "D" Coy on right on night 8/9th and "D" moved to point in Support "C" Coy withdrawing into Reserve in BUTLER AVENUE.

**Sept. 9.** At 10.40 a.m. on 9th "A" Coy reported being established on Line BUTLER SUPPORT - IRON TRENCH to Q.3.c.80.92 thence North Westwards towards "B" Coy. "B" Coy pushed forward along LEAD STREET and OXFORD ALLEY and also established line SHROPSHIRE TRENCH and BUTLER TRENCH. They were not in touch with 8th Lincolns on left until 12.30 p.m. 8th Lincolns moving up LEAD STREET from SHROPSHIRE RESERVE at 12 noon.
About 4.30 p.m. a Machine Gun Post was captured at BUTLER CROSS and right Company pushed on Eastwards from this point along TRESSAULT TRENCH which was evacuated in a hurry, some 16 of the enemy with three Machine Guns being just caught sight of as they escaped to Trenches Q.4.c.75.60. They were followed from about Q.3.b.2.1.
The left Company succeeded in pushing down TUNNEL AVENUE to QUEER STREET and thence Westwards through scrubb to about Q.3.b.9.9. but could not get further, there being no trench and our line up to this point being only a series of posts. The attempt to push forward along SYKE ALLEY met with no success, the Trench being very open and entirely under observation. The night being very dark, it was decided to complete the capture of the rest of our objective until dawn on 10th when the rest of the position was made good.
It is worthy to mention that QUEER STREET exists practically only in name, the trench where it does exist being over-grown and filled with wire except immediately East and West of TUNNEL AVENUE.
During the 9th, 10th and 11th th enemy subjected the whole of the area Q.3. to heavy shelling sending over a good deal of gas Blue and Yellow Cross.
On being informed that we were to be relieved by 2/5th West Riding Regt, who were to attack at dawn on 12th September, Patrols were sent out by left Front Line Company to ascertain the position of wire opposite the Front and detailed information was obtained and communicated. Gaps in this wire were cut and marked by the Battalion and handing over report was sent to O.C. West Riding Regt.

In conclusion I wish to lay stress on the fact that the advance was carried out by relying on manoeuvre rather than fire power. Invariably the enemy on finding himself out-flanked and in danger of being cut off, retired hurriedly. This was the case at each successive bound when enemy posts were seen to withdraw by our advanced troops on their flanks. On at least two occasions a large number of prisoners would have been taken had not fire been opened by the enemy on the flank which served as a warning to ~~xxxxxxxxxxxx~~ the enemy to withdraw as he invariably did.

The value of finding definite Company Headquarters ahead of time for each bound, and of maintaining a forward Battalion report centre connected by telephone was clearly demonstrated.

The importance of advancing by bounds and establishing touch all along the line before again advancing was clearly seen.

The rapidity of an advance depends largely on not having to throw back a flank.

The success of open Warfare fighting of this kind depends upon the initiative and enterprise of Junior Officers and N.C.O's.

I wish to give credit to the Company Officers, N.C.O's and men for their conduct during operations of a difficult nature new to the very great majority.

The following casualties were suffered by the Battalion:-

|  | Killed. | Wounded. | Injured Gas. | Missing. |
|---|---|---|---|---|
| Officers. | - | 3 | -- | -- |
| Other Ranks: | 7 | * 57 | 36 | -- |

\* 3 of these have since died of Wounds.

C.J.o.B.Meringham
Lt.Colonel.
16.9.18.   Commanding 8th (S) Bn Somerset Light Infantry.

To:- O.C. "C" Coy.

Push out Patrols all along your front with a view to establishing a line further forward except on the right at Road Junction P.6.d. 20.65 where the double Lewis Gun Section will remain and cover Southern prolongation of sunken roads with look-out posts slightly forward and on top of Eastern Bank,so as to command approaches along Sunken Road.

Wire will be sent up to you and a double apron will be erected across Sunken Road 35 yards South of Southern post. With your 3rd Platoon you will echelon back your Right Flank by establishing two posts to connect up with "D" Coy at P.6.c.5.5. The remaining platoon will be held in Reserve in Sunken Road along with your Headquarters at P.6.b.10.15.

Your front posts will be numbered from R. to L. taking up next number to "D" Coy who will number his right post One. I am moving one platoon from "B" Company to take up position in reserve to you at P.5.b. On western side of wire, please keep in touch with them and have them reconnoitre your Headquarters and Line.

6.9.18.  H.C.PRING CAPT & ADJT.
0.30 a.m.  8th (S) Bn Somerset Light Infantry.

---

To:- O's C. "A", "B", "C", &"D"

General Officers Commanding Brigades of 63rd New Zealand Division are considering the advisability of establishing the line on Western Edge of HAVRINCOURT WOOD. There is a possibility of Orders being received to advance over line to Western Edge of Wood under a Barrage which would deal with enemy posts on Western edge of Wood. Early information should be sent in of any enemy posts established forward of the Wood, so that these may be dealt with, otherwise advance under barrage might result in severe losses.

7.9.18.  H.C.PRING CAPT & ADJT.
2 a.m.  8th (S) Bn Somerset Light Infantry.

---

To:- O's C. "A" & "B" Coys.

Should the further Objective referred to in Order No. 95,not be undertaken by you on completion of the first objective; this second operation will probably have to be undertaken in the afternoon as it could not be left till the evening, it being considered absolutely vital to future operations that the QUEER STREET objective should be gained before dawn on the 10th inst which means that it could not be left until dusk on the 9th.

The thing to be avoided of course, is an operation conducted under good observation conditions for the enemy when his sniping Batteries might inflict heavy casualties on us and render our forward positions untenable. Once gained QUEEN STREET should be held with about half a dozen strong points not necessarily in trench but above all, concealed. All ranks should be warned of the great danger to all concerned of movement during daylight on the 9th.

9.9.18  H.C.PRING CAPT & ADJT.
1 a.m.  8th (S) Bn Somerset Light Infantry.

ORDERS ISSUED TO COMPANIES DURING OPERATIONS
3.9.18. to 11.9.18.
------------------------------------------------

To:- All Companies.

"D" Coy will push slowly forward its two leading platoons to a position just, not under observation by the enemy, on east ridge running through P.3.a. pushing forward scouts to positions from which observation of ground can be had N. & W. of HAVRINCOURT WOOD.

"C" Coy will conform with two platoons along line through J.33.c. with scouts forward.

"B" Coy will replace "C" Coy in their present position in J.33.c. & D. and "A" Coy will replace "D" in P.3.a. and J.33.c.

Battalion Headquarters will move to J.31d.2.2.

Forward Report Centre now established in P.3.a, in charge of Lieut. AUSTIN.

Visual communication is being established from this point. Report your Headquarters "C" & "D" Coys in moving forward will avoid observation by enemy.

ACKNOWLEDGE.               H.C.PRING CAPT & ADJT.
                              8th (S) Bn Somerset L.I.
3.9.18.
12.30 p.m. N.C.
------------------------------------------------

To:- O.C. "D" Coy.

It is reported by "C" Coy that an effort was made last night by the enemy to cut off and do in their post at P.6.d.30.80.

This attempt was made from the direction of P.6.d.1.5.

Herewith copy of Orders to "C" Coy.

The ground has been reconnoitred by the Commanding Officer early this morning when the light was good. There is no difficulty about establishing posts diagonally from P.6.Central to P.6.c.0.0. There are several old huts and shelters which could be occupied with perfect safety affording good observation.

From this line of posts two or three patrols working together might be pushed forward towards probable enemy posts in neighbourhood of P.15.a.3.6. by working quitly forward as soon as dark; these patrols might find southern end of Sunken Road unoccupied and by laying in ambush should be able, without difficulty, during the night to scupper any enemy who might enter Sunken Road.

Patrolling should be active and every effort should be made to locate enemy s o that the ~~artillery~~ artillery may be informed with a view to harrassing the enemy with good results.

Daylight observation posts should be established and scouts will be sent forward to use for this purpose.

6.9.18.                    H.C.PRING CAPT & ADJT.
9.30 a.m.                  8th (S) Bn Somerset Light Infantry.

OPERATION ORDERS
No.94                                    7.9.18.
8th (S) Bn Somerset Light Infantry.   Headquarters.

There is every indication that the enemy is evacuating HAVRINCOURT WOOD.
The Battalion has advanced to Front Line so that it now lies approximately between Q.7.c.50.10 and Q.1.d.70.80 along track running N.E. and S.W. to
At 5.15 a.m. today "C" & "D" Coys will continue their advance.
Their Boundaries are as follows:-
On the N. a line drawn East & West through Q.2.central on the S. from Q.7. out along track to Q.8.c.00.50 thence to PLACE MORTIMARD Q.8.d.25.70 thence Q. East.
Inter-Company boundary place ST.HUBERT - CLAYTON CROSS thence S.E. Q.8.a.35.65.
"D" Coy will continue advance on right and "C" on left.
O.C. "B" Coy will assemble two platoons at P.12.b.85.50 and two platoons Q7.a.30.99 under Command of 2/Lt.FORD.
These two platoons in each case will be prepared to move, the first two, to PLACE MORTIMARD and second two to CLAYTON CROSS on receipt of instructions from O.C. "D" & "C" Coys respectively.
O.C. "A" Coy will move forward the Company at 6 a.m. on 7th inst. to trenches and posts in P.11.b.
At this hour O.C.Coys 4th Middlesex Regt. attached, will move forward their Companies to trenches in P.10.b. and P.4.d. and will send Orderlies to forward Battalion Report Centre at P.12.b.32.60.
Battalion Headquarters is now at P.11.b.00.20
Forward Report Centre is being established at P.12.b.60.60
O.C. "A" Coy will send two Orderlies to forward Report Centre at 6 a.m.
"C" Section Machine Gun Battalion will report with two Guns at Battalion Headquarters at 6.a.m.
O.C.Coys in continuing their advance will do so in depth, touch will be maintained with the enemy whose rear-guards will be harrassed as much as possible.
Upon meeting with any determined resistance Map co-ordnance of enemy post lines will at once be sent back to Battalion report centre in order that the artillery may be informed.
Companies will be responsible that touch is maintained on their flanks throughout and will report where their Headquarters is established.as they move forward.

ACKNOWLEDGE BY BEARER.

Issued at 1.a.m.


                    C.T.de B.SHERINGHAM, Lt.Colonel.
              Commanding 8th (S) Bn Somerset Light Infantry.

He should aim at being at this point at 6 a.m.9.9.18 and if the advance is continued will inform O.C. of "D" Coy who will at once move One platoon into TUFNELL AVENUE in Q.3.d. and One Platoon to OXFORD ALLEY.

The advance of the Battalion from the line SHROPSHIRE TRENCH - BUTLER TRENCH and TUFNELL AVENUE will not be attempted until this line is established.

The further objective as far north as QUEER STREET and as far as BURNLEY ALLEY "D" SAP will have to be undertaken by the Battalion and its capture and consolidation must be completed by dawn on the 10th inst.

Unless O's C. "A" & "B" Coys on meeting at Q.3.c.80.9.8 are satisfied that the further advance can at once be undertaken and the ground made good, this second objective will be undertaken separately.

It should be remembered that QUEER STREET and SYKE ALLEY are in-different Trenches very much over-looked from HAVRINCOURT and on the forward slope.

Should however, atmospheric conditions be propitious and visibility poor on completion of the capture of the first objective, this operation should be continued at once.

O.C. "D" Coy will responsible for reporting to advanced Battalion Report Centre at CLAYTON CROSS progress of the operations.

Lieut H.K.AUSTIN will be at CLAYTON CROSS from 6.30 a.m. onwards.

O's C. "A" & "B" Coy should report to O.C. "D" Coy by runner to Cross Roads at Q.2.b.95.60.

The position when taken will be held by a series of strong posts sited so as to command the approaches.

O.C."C" Coy will remain in his present position and will keep in close touch with report centre at CLAYTON CROSS.

ACKNOWLEDGE BY BEARER.

H.O.PRING CAPT & ADJT for LT.COL.
Commanding 8th (S) Bn Somerset Light Infantry.

OPERATION ORDERS
No.95                                    9.9.18.
8th (S) Bn Somerset Light Infantry.   Headquarters.

1 a.m.

Orders have been received that the Battalion has to occupy before the morning of the 10th a position as follows:-

Bounded on the north by QUEER STREET running through Q.3.a. & b. and Q.4.a. as far West as the Junction of QUEER STREET with SYKE ALLEY.

The position to be bounded on the East by BURNLEY ALY "D" Sap.

The position on the South will be bounded by TRESCAULT SUPPORT as far East as Q.4.c.25.85 as far West as its Junction with TUFNELL AVENUE thence South to Q.3.d.1.5.

The southern Battalion Boundary will be the Grid Line East and West to the North of Q.3. and K.33

8th Bn Lincolnshire Regt. will be to the north of the Battalion from the Junction of SYKE ALLEY and QUEER STREET N.W. along trench.

4th Bn Middlesex Regt. will be to the South.

4th Bn Middlesex Regt. will relieve "D" Coy in TUFNELL AVENUE and QUADRANGLE TRENCH under arrangements to be notified separately.

The Battalion is now disposed as follows:-

"D" Coy from about Q.3.c.05.70 to Q.9.a.45.70 with Supports about PLACE MORTIMARD.

"A" Coy from Q.9.a.45.70 along TUFNELL AVENUE as far as Q.3/d.1.5. with a flank t hrown back at Q.3.c.70.30 to meet "B" Coy at about Q.3.c.30.40.

"B" Coy are responsible from Q.3.c.30.40 to Q.3.d.65.99. At dawn on 9.9.18 Patrols will be pushed out by "A" Coy North along TUFNELL AVENUE.

By "B" Coy along OXFORD ALLEY and Lead Street.

These Patrols will aim at the establishment of the line TUFNELL AVENUE and BUTLER TRENCH and SHROPSHIRE TRENCH as far North as the East and West Grid Line to the North of Q.2. Patrols will therefore be supported in strength.

On reaching BUTLER TRENCH O.C. "B" Coy will work from OXFORD ALLEY S.Eastwards along BUTLER TRENCH as far as Q.3.c.80.98. He will also make certain that there are no Troops of the enemy in BUTLER SUPPORT.

O.C. "B" Coy on reaching junction of SHROPSHIRE TRENCH and LEAD STREET will proceed S.E. along SHROPSHIRE TRENCH as far as Q.3.a.30.50

"A" & "B" Coy Commanders will meet at Q.3.c.80.98 to report mutually that this operation has been successfully completed.

The next Line to be made good will be undertaken by O.C. "A" & "B" Coys as follows:-

"A" Coy will responsible for establishing the line QUEER STREET, East of the Junction of QUEER STREET and TUFNELL AVENUE Q.3.b.80.75 and will make good the Eastern part of the Battalion objective as far east as BURNLEY "D" Sap and pushing East along TRESCAULT TRENCH and TRESCAULT SUPPORT.

O.C. "B" Coy will work North of SYKE ALLEY as far as QUEER STREET and thence East along QUEER STREET and thence along QUEER STREET as far as the junction of QUEER STREET and TUFNELL AVENUE.

O.C. "D" Coy will send an Officer to follow "A" Coy from Q.3.d.1.5. and to meet O's C. "A" & "B" Coys at Q.3.c.80.98.

OPERATION ORDER
No.96                                          11.9.18.
8th (S) Bn Somerset Light Infantry.    Headquarters

1. **RELIEF.** The Battalion is being relieved tonight by 2/5th West Riding Regt.

2. **ORDER OF RELIEF.** "D" Coy West Riding Regt on Right.
"B"   "      "      "      "    Left.

O's C. "A" & "B" Coy will leave their existing outpost line from K.33.c.55.25 to along QUEER STREET to Q.4.a.30.57 and the post at Q.4.a.15.10 and Q.4.a.05.05 and supporting post to each of these last two. It is possible that the platoon of "A" Coy in TRESCAULT TRENCH and TRESCAULT SUPPORT may be relieved by troops of the 111th Infantry Brigade.

The rest of the Battalion will withdraw as follows:- "A", "B", & "D" Coys upon arrival in position of "B" & "D" Coys 2/5th West Riding Regt to LEBUCQUIERE Extras.I.30.a.

"C" Coy will withdraw from its present position at 9 p.m. and proceed to new area.

The troops left in the Outpost Line will be withdrawn at ZERO minus One hour and will rejoin the Battalion.

ZERO hour will be notified later.

3. **GUIDES.** Companies will be met by Guides at LEBUCQUIERE Cross Roads in I.30b. 20.80

"A" & "B" Coys will each send 5 guides to be at the Cross Roads Q.8.b.9.6. at 7.30 p.m. to act as guides for "B" & "D" Coys 2/5th West Riding Regt into position in BUTLER TRENCH & BUTLER SUPPORT.

"D" Coy will detail 2 Other Ranks to be at PLACE MORTEMARD at 9.30 p.m. to guide Transport of 2nd/5th West Riding Regt. to the present ration Dump at about Q.3.c.65.45.

4. **ROUTE.** MATHESON ROAD - RUYAULCOURT.

5. **CONFERENCE.** O's C. "A" & "B" Coys will report to O.C. 2/5th West Riding Regt. at present "A" Coys HdQrs Q.3.a.05.10. at 8.30 p.m.

6. **TAPES AND WIRE.** O.C. "B" Coy will arrange with incoming Company Commanders to lay out tapes to the last belt of our defensive wire cutting gaps in any belts up to that point. The laying out of these tapes and the cutting of the wire will be undertaken as late as is thought possible but this should be reconnoitred unless today's patrols can undertake this work.

An Officer will be detailed by O.C. "B" Coy to show incoming Officers our line of posts between SHROPSHIRE SPUR ROAD and the ROAD running from HAVRINCOURT through Q.3.a.65.99.

7. **TRANSPORT.** Each Company will send a Guide for Lewis Gun Limber to be at the report centre at 9 p.m.

All Lewis Guns, Magazines, Petrol Tins Etc., will be sent back on these limbers.

8. **COOKS.** A hot meal will be provided for the men on arrival in new Billets.

9. REPORT.     Completion of relief will be notified to
present Battalion H.Q. by Phone or Runner using
the words "YOUR A.B.1 RECEIVED"
       A similar report will be rendered on arrival
in new area using the word "THANKS".

10. BATTALION H.Q.
         New Battalion H.Q. will be at I.30.a.3.6.


                    H.O.PRING CAPT & ADJT.
           8th (S) Bn Somerset Light Infantry.


          No.96/1 ADDITIONAL OPERATION ORDER TO No.96.
                    dated 11.9.18.
          ============================================

1. ZERO.      ZERO hour will be at 5.25 a.m. 12.9.18.

2. OUTPOSTS.  The platoons in the outpost Line which are
      left behind will come out as formed parties each
      platoon under its own officer and will report at
      Battalion H.Q. P.6.d.2.6. on the way down.

3. ACCOMMODATION.  ~~xxxxxxxxxxxxxxxx~~ (LEBUCQUIERE)
              "A" Coy I.30.a.90.90.
              "B"  "  I.30.b.20.80
              "C"  "  I.24.d.50.40.
              "D"  "  I.30.d.50.90.


11.9.18.
8.30 p.m.        H.O.PRING CAPT & ADJT.
            8th (S) Bn Somerset Light Infantry.

## HANDING OVER REPORT.

To:- Officer Commanding
    2/5th West Riding Regt.

1. Herewith Sketch showing our dispositions at moment of handing over.
   This shows disposition of:-
   (a) Infantry.
   (b) Machine Guns.
   (c) Trench Mortars.

2. Touch is established with Unit on left ( 8th Bn. Lincolnshire Regt.) at K.33.c.8.2.
                                        at K.33.c.3.0.
                                        at Q.3.a.2.6.
   Touch is established on right with (4th Bn. Middlesex Regt.) at Q.4.b.2.1.

3. COMMUNICATIONS.
   Bde H.Q. P.11.b.9.2.        Battn. P.6.d.2.6.
   4th Middlesex P.6.d.3.7.    8th Lincolns. Q.1.a.2.5.
   M.G.C.   Q.7.a.1.5.
   Station at CLAYTON CROSS - Q.9.a.9.7.
   Coy.H.Q. Q.3.b.05.10.

4. BATTALION ADVANCED REPORT CENTRE. - Q.9.a.9.7.

5. S.O.S. RELAY STATION and Permanent Sentry Post established at Q.9.a.9.7.

6. ROUTES TO FRONT LINE. The best Route is from WOOD PLACE Q.1.a.05.10 - CLAYTON CROSS - Q.9.a.9.7. thence by either
   (1) SHROPSHIRE SPUR ROAD to BUTLER CROSS or
   (2) QUADRANGLE TRENCH - OXFORD ALLEY or
   (3) TUNNEL AVENUE.

7. The enemy has good observation of the area from HAVRINCOURT and from TRESCAULT.

8. OBSERVATION OF THE ENEMY. T.M's at K.33.a.25.80 - K.33.b.05.60 + M.G's at Q.4.a.80.55 and trench eastwards also in trench immediately North of Q.4.a.80.55. Much movement at K.33.b.05.60 and along Sunken Road westwards.

9. Patrol reports for wire and ground opposite our front not yet to hand. Company Commanders will hand over any information to hand.

10. RATIONS. By limber along road from Q.9.a.0.7. thence along SHROPSHIRE SPUR ROAD to about Q.3.c.20.60 where limbers are met and carrying parties collect.

11. WATER. By Petrol Tins.

12. DUG-OUTS. At following points:- Q.8.a.10.20 - Q.8.a.30.30.
    Q.9.a.0.7. - Q.3.b.05.10 - Q.3.a.20.50 - Q.3.b.30.10
    Q.9.a.30.85 - Q.3.a.Central - Q.3.c.80.50.

13. ARTILLERY.
    Am not giving details owing to circumstances of handing over.

4.9.18.                         C.J.de B. SHERINGHAM. Lt.Colonel.
                        Commanding 8th (S) Bn Somerset Light Infantry.

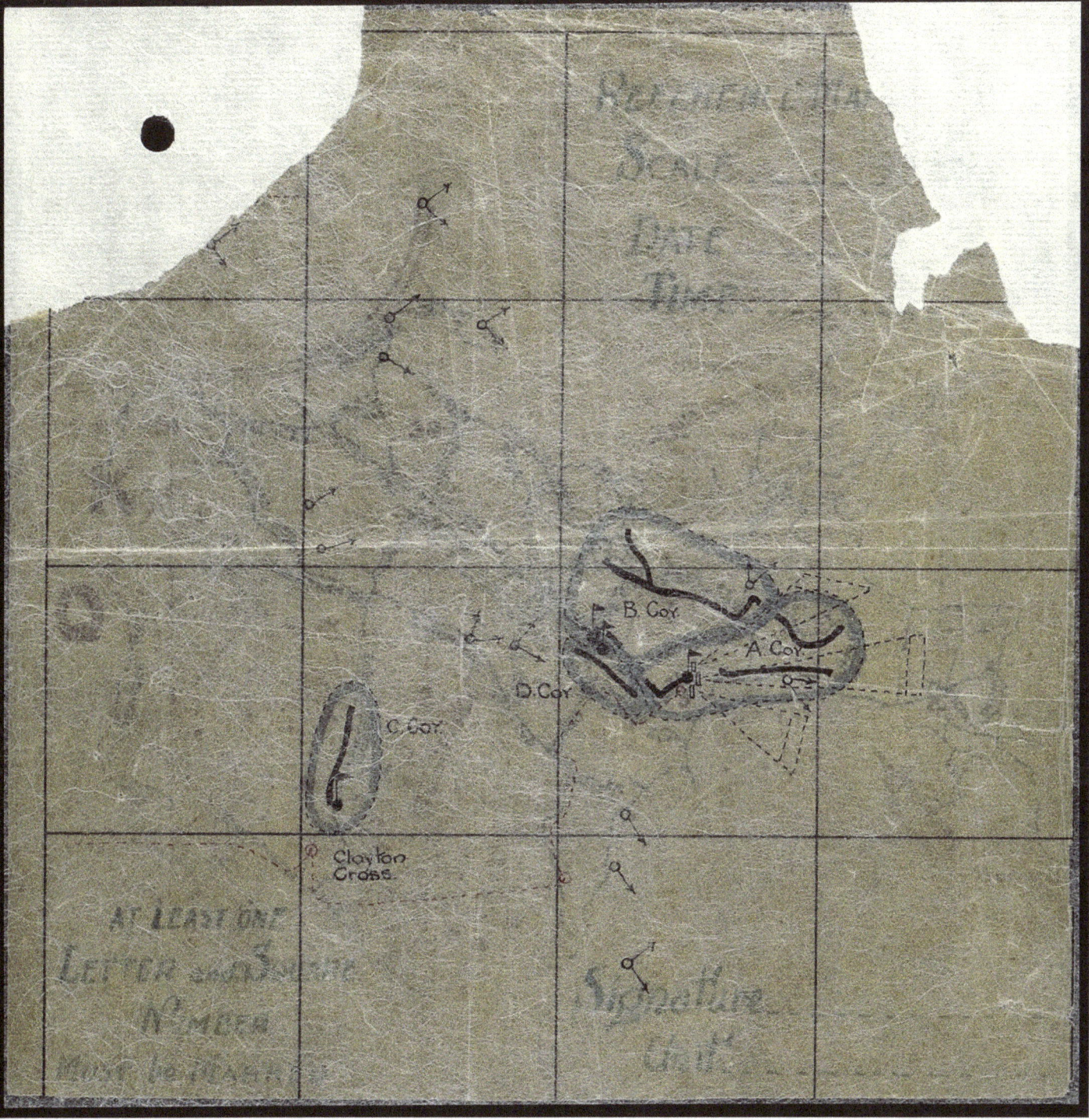

63rd Brigade.
37th Division.

8th BATTALION

THE SOMERSET LIGHT INFANTRY

OCTOBER 1918

WAR DIARY for
October 1918.

PART 1

| Hour, Date, Place | Summary of Events and Information | Remarks and references to Appendices |
|---|---|---|

30.9.18.   On relief of 5th Division by the 37th Division the Battalion moved to S.E. Corner of HAVRINCOURT WOOD.

5.10.18.   At 19.00 hours moved to valley north GOUZEAUCOURT.

7.10.18.   At 17.30 hours moved to area immediately South of GOUZEAUCOURT – CAMBRAI ROAD in HINDENBURG Line R.23 Sheet 57 c S.E.

8.10.18.   At 05.30 hours moved vca BANTEUX Canal Bridge near Factory M.29.c.2.2. BANTOUZELLE to HINDENBURG Support Line in M.27, arriving there about 07.15 hours.
         At 15.00 hours received orders to move forward to Assembly Position South of PELU WOOD N.8.central. These orders were changed and at 15.15 hours orders were received to go straight through to position on line BOUT DU PRE – CROSS ROADS N.4.c.0.3. for an attack at 18.00 hours in South Easterly direction, Bearing 130 true, with object of securing high ground in N.11 & N.5. Lincolns on left.
         At 17.00 hours received orders that attack was changed from 18.00 hours to 18.30 hrs and that Battalion would form up on similar line in N.4.c. with Lincolns on Right instead of left. and a Barrage on line N.10.a.9.8. to N.4.d.7.2. and pivoting on this line until it was sweeping East to Sunken Road running North and South in N.5. and N.11.
         (At 19 hours telephonic communication established between PELU WOOD and Sunken Road N.5.b.7.5. and Forward Brigade Report Centre at N.W. Corner of BRISEUX WOOD)
         The Battalion reached its Assembly positions at dusk and moved off at ZERO, but advance under the Barrage was rendered most difficult owing to the action of either one or two batteries, casualties being inflicted on our own troops, whose advance was thrown out and greatly delayed in consequence. Upon these batteries ceasing however, the advance was resumed and a line taken up running from about N.5.b.4.4. to N.11.b.2.9. thence South West across GUILLEMIN – BOUT DU PRE ROAD at about N.11.c.4.7. touch being obtained with 6th Lincolns at about N.11.c.1.8.
         The Farm at N.11.a.3.9. which held up our advance at first was entered and occupied at about 01.00 hours October 9th.

                                        G.L. Cherrington
                                        Lt. Colonel.
         Commanding 6th (S) Bn. Somerset Light Infantry.

(1)

### WAR DIARY or INTELLIGENCE SUMMARY

Army Form C. 2118.

| Hour, Date, Place | Summary of Events and Information | Remarks and references to Appendices |
|---|---|---|
| | At 13.30 hours orders were received that the advance was to be continued at 05.20 hours, barrage starting at on Line N.17.c.75.80 – H.35.d.t.0. objective HAUCOURT High ground G7.d. This necessitated sending out at once and withdrawing companies to a position of Assembly along line of Sunken Road from N.5.d.0.5. to Road Junction N.5.a.2.7. Issued verbal orders for an attack on a Three-Company front, each Company to be in depth – "D" Coy on left, "A" Coy in centre and "B" Coy on Right. "C" Coy to follow in Close Support. | |
| | This formation was chosen as 4th Middlesex were in close Support. Companies reached their positions of Assembly at about 05.00 hours | |
| 9.10.18. | ZERO hours for the attack was fixed at 05.20 hrs. Companies moved forward under cover of Artillery barrage. New Zealanders co-operating on the left, a Company of the 4th Middlesex coming up on our right. | |
| | A delay of half an hour was occasioned about 150 yards before reaching the Eastern outskirts of HAUCOURT owing to two Batteries firing short. No opposition was met with from the enemy. | |
| | A line was established running North and South through I.31. 113th Brigade passing through 63rd Infantry Brigade to exploit the success to CAUDRY. | |
| | BATTALION HEADQUARTERS was established at HAUCOURT in the course of the afternoon about 17.00 hrs. Companies were joined by Cookers and a hot meal was taken at 01.30 hours. | |
| 10.10.18. | Moved at 06.30 hours and assembled in I.32.a. and at about 08.15 hours moved forward through I.33.a.& b. and I.34.a. & b. Road in I.35.a. crossing Railway to J.13.c. & d. waiting thereat for about One hour. A track had to be reconnoitred for transport as Roads were blown up and rendered impassable in places | |
| | 10.00 hours moved to Practice Trenches in J.19.b. 12.10 hours sent on "A" Coy to act as an advance guard. | |
| | 13.00 Hours moved to PT CAUDRY where Battn. was concentrated – "A" Coy to report progress making Coy Headquarters successively PT CAUDRY – CLERMONT CHATEAU and Road Junction at J.4.central. | |
| | Conference of Company Commanders at PT CAUDRY at 14.30 hours. | |
| | Orders received at about 14.00 hours to go through 113th Infantry Brigade, meantime "A" Coy by 14.15 hours was a long way through, 113th Brigade having connected up with New Zealanders at about D.30.central and with 17th Division at E.19.1.4.1. | |
| | As Brigade Orders directed 6th Lincolns to advance on our Right, word was sent to O.C. "A" Coy to close on his left and sent "B" Coy up to take over Right Battalion Front, "D" Coy in Support "C" Coy in Reserve at J.4.Central. | |
| | At about 17.00 hours the Battalion advanced to the attack on the Ridge D.30 – J.6. | |
| | As the distance seemed not to be covered by the two Companies and as the New Zealanders were not advancing on our left "D" Coy was ordered to move forward in the centre and "A" Coy directed to work North Eastwards. | |

*signature*
Lt Colonel.
Commanding 6th (S) Bn Somerset Light Infantry.

The advance went on in spite of heavy Machine Gun and Artillery fire - the enemy were holding the high ground with a few light Machine gun posts which by individual Section enterprise and initiative were either killed or forced to retire or taken prisoners.

The Machine Gun and Artillery barrage was very heavy and CAPT.C.H.MADDEN.M.C. was severely wounded in the head. On reaching crest, orders were given for the leading wave to dig in at once on the reverse slope, with several observation posts on the forward slope.

The waning light was chiefly responsible for avoiding serious casualties which would certainly have occurred, had the observation for enemy artillery observers remained good.

The left flank meanwhile, being in the air, one platoon of the Reserve Company was sent to form a defensive flank as a temporary measure until the leading Companies were re-organized in depth.

The New Zealand Division right flank was near J.4.Central. They agreed to push forward and join up with our refused flank.

By about 20.00 hours the line was established Reserve Company Platoon withdrawn, left Company with flank thrown back to connect up with New Zealanders and all three leading Companies re-organized in depth.

All Companies were ordered to send out strong patrols to reconnoitre and report on any available crossing over River SELLE.

These patrols reported at about 22.00 hours that no Crossings were available and that the River SELLE was from 20 - 30 feet in width and that there were no trees which could be felled across the river.

11.10.18. At about 23.00 hours it was arranged with 2/Lt.KEITH of 153 Coy R.E's that he would try and erect some sort of Bridge. "B" & "D" Coy Commanders and One Company 8th Lincolns to hold 3 platoons in readiness to proceed across river if ordered to do so. 2/Lt.H.W.BROOKS commanding "A" Coy and One Platoon of "A" Coy pushed on to reconnoitre and if possible occupy BRIASTRE. Though some of the enemy were still in the village and were taken prisoners on the following morning, they met with no opposition and fell in with the New Zealanders (1st Wellington Battalion) in the Middle of BRIASTRE just about Divisional Boundary and decided to push on across river by a bridge which was found had just been completed by 2/Lt.BALDER of 153 Field Coy R.E's.

2/Lt.BROOKS went back to fetch his Company down into BRIASTRE and to send word to O.C. "B" Coy and "D" Coy and 8th Lincolns Company to send on their platoons down Sunken Road to Cross river, and took platoon on across river with New Zealanders who took over two complete Companies, and worked north on our left. The Commanding Officer who had gone forward with 2nd Lt.BROOKS, then returned across River, met and conducted back across river the remaining two platoons and one Platoon 8th Lincolns and pointed out their positions, it being light enough to see 200 or 300 yards. He then returned and found the ridge held by "B" & "D" Coy, each less one Platoon and then returned to Headquarters.

During the 11th enemy Machine Gun and Snipers were very active from Railway and our men being w

Lt.Colonel
Comdg. 8th (S) Bn Somerset Light Infantry.

quickly and only returned at about 14.00 hours when he reported it impossible to get any men out across river in daylight. Meantime at 14.00 hours Headquarters moved forward and three platoons "C" Company to EPIASTRE getting all 70 men over forward slopes and into cellar accomodation without casualties by trickling them down.

At 15.45 hours the enemy counter attacked heavily and careful watch was kept of the railway and road in case enemy should attempt to debouch and move forward against EPIASTRE or attack our troops on East side of River.

No enemy movement being seen, the two companies were kept in cellars until dusk and in spite of the heavy shelling suffered no casualties at this time.

Between 17.00 and 17.45 hours "A" Coy moved out of cellars, crossed river by EASTERN Bridge and reinforced 4th Middlesex at E.15.a.0.3. along Sunken Road.

("B" Coy on arrival at about 18.00 hours in accordance with Orders telephoned to Rear H.Qrs were ordered to take up position along Sunken Road further South, On right of "A" Coy and One Company 1/1st Herts remained as Reserve in EPIASTRE)

At 17.30 hours orders were received from G.O.C. 63rd Infantry Brigade that New Zealanders were attacking BULLY VUE at 18.00 hours and we were to co-operate. "C" Coy at once moved off to take up position occupied by it on previous night from 01.30 to 04.45 hours and to attack with New Zealanders.

CAPT. AQUITMAN M.C. also co-operated with a trench mortar which he established and handled most skillfully, firing on houses and railway in vicinity of BULLY VUE.

The attack was successful in the neighbourhood LA BULLY VUE, and no casualties had been incurred by this Battalion in the course of this attack, and it was decided to attempt to exploit our success Southwards.

The length of front held by the attacking Company was about 200 yards commencing with a post in close touch with the New Zealanders at LA BULLE VUE. Two platoons of another Company pushed Southwards along the railway cutting and with the assistance of a further platoon of another Company established a line of posts in the Railway along a frontage of 800 yards.

The weather conditions and extreme blackness of the night together with the difficulty of having to mop dug-outs on the East side of Western Railway embankment, with the responsibility of handing over the position sufficiently mopped up to new troops, and the danger of establishing a line of posts too lightly held in the vicinity of an embankment containing dug-outs all along; the difficulty of establishing a good line further South and also the knowledge of the proposed disposition of the incoming Unit, decided me not to attempt to consolidate the whole railway along the divisional front.

*Jack Kennington*
Lt. Colonel.
Commanding 8th (S) Bn Somerset Light Infantry.

under cover of deep Sunken Bank and Sunken Road suffered no casualties east of the STYLE.

Further bridges were erected during the night and orders were received that 4th Middlesex were to relieve the Battalion East of River and attack at 03.00 hours.

Meanwhile New Zealanders were also attacking and word received from O.C. 1st Wellington Battalion that he had received orders to attack with his right on Factory D.34.d.5.1. and would require to be relieved in the position on our left East of RIVER. Accordingly "C" Coy was sent forward to reconnoitre and take over his position.

This relief was completed at about 01.30 hours.

Companies were relieved on the East side of the River by 4th Middlesex by 04.45 hours and then withdrew as ordered west of the Ridge J.6. - D.30. except that "A" Coy and part of "C" Coy were kept in BRIASTRE in cellars.

The attack of 4th Middlesex was successful on the right, but on the left it was held up by the enemy from neighbourhood of BELLE VUE.

At about 07.30 hours the Commanding Officer saw Officer Commanding 4th Middlesex, who seemed satisfied with the situation, and offered to send up my Company in BRIASTRE in Support to his left if he wished, as messages had been received shewing situation on left to be obscure, but he did not encourage this being done.

At 07.40 hours the situation was discussed with Brigade Major who agreed situation required troops sent forward - One Company 1/1st Herts sent up with guide furnished by this Battalion to E.25.a.2.2. in Support to 4th Middlesex.

Word received that this Company on going forward came under Machine Gun fire from Railway. On this account and on further word being received later, confirming occupation of Railway by enemy near E.25 central and further north, it was decided to try and get troops over river and into railway further South near Cemetry NEUVILLY. This Plan was approved by Brigade and another Company FOZA was placed at our disposal at 12 noon. This Company under 2/Lt. FRYER was then sent and "B" Coy of this Battalion with One Mortar to cross River by crossing in K.1.c.

They attempted to cross in very extended formation (Section in Worms) but came at once under heavy Machine Gun Fire not only from N.E. but also from direction of NEUVILLY and were forced to withdraw to Road in J.6.a. & b.

Consequently this, which was the main effort to restore the situation on left flank failed and no word of this was received until about 16.00 hrs

Word was sent at 12.00 hours to O.C. "A" Coy to get his Company across river and take up a position from which he could co-operate with the advance northwards along railway by "B" Coy and FOZA Company.

He at once went out to reconnoitre and getting across river obtained the disposition of 4th Middlesex and New Zealanders. Owing to the incessant Rifle fire and Machine Guns fire by the enemy from Railway he was not able to move

*[signature]*
Lt. Colonel.
Commanding 6th (S) Bn Somerset Light Infantry.

The flank therefore was thrown back at the only satisfactory point i.e. Practice trenches in E.25.c. thence to steep sunken xxxx Bank echeloned back South West and the sunken road as far South as hedge running due East and West at E.25.c.6.1.

An Officer's fighting patrol did, however, reconnoitre the Railway for a further 150 yards South of our Right S post as shown on map attached and met with no opposition. He however, reported an enemy machine Gun post at point where sunken Road cuts railway E.25.b.7.1. and lights were being fired from Railway further South.

The Wire West of the Railway consisted of 3 fences about 5 yards apart at a distance of some 15 yards from the West bank of the Railway.

The Battalion was relieved by 16th Royal Warwickshire Regt., relief being completed at about 03.30 hours on October 13th.

Thanks of the Battalion are due to Majors THORNE & McDONALD Commanding Battery "D" 123 Brigade and 4.5.How.Battery respectively, whose co-operation with the Infantry was of the greatest possible value.

We owe to the enterprise of 153 Field Coy R.E's in constructing bridges across the River SELLE our ability to cross the River on night of 10th October.

Credit is due to all ranks for their behaviour in the attack on Ridge D.30 - J.6. and for their endurance on night October 8th/9th when they were in action all night and until about 11.00 hours the following morning after marching from about 14.30 hours to their assembly position.

The conduct of all concerned on night 11th 12th during and following the Counter-attack on BELLE VUE was most creditable.

13.10.18. The Battalion on being relieved by the 16th Battn. Royal Warwickshire, moved back to CAUDRY in Billets. Training was carried out here until 21st October.

23.10.18. The Battalion moved to VIESLY and the same day moved further forward to BRIASTRE occupying billets there for the night.

24.10.18. Battalion moved into the Line.

31.10.18. A Raid was carried out by the 6th .Somerset.L.I. See "Report on Raid" and Operation Orders X.Z.2.attached.

**WEATHER DURING MONTH.**
Exceptionally fine and dry and favourable for operations.

*C.J.Buckingham*
Lt.Colonel.
Commanding 6th(S) Bn.Somerset Light Infantry.

PART II

| Hour, Date, Place | Summary of Events and Information | Remarks and references to Appendices |
|---|---|---|
| 2.10.18. | The Corps Commander, under authority granted by His Majesty the KING, awarded the following decoration to the undernamed for conspicuous gallantry and devotion to duty near HAVRINCOURT 9/10th Sept 1918.<br><br>THE MILITARY MEDAL.<br>No.30919 Pte. E.T.Herbert.<br>No.304039 Pte. S.C.GILES<br>No.38445 Pte. H.MITCHELL.<br><br>Nine (9) Other Ranks joined the Battalion. | |
| 3.10.18. | Major C.J.PEARD D.S.O. proceeded to England to attend a Course at Aldershot.<br><br>Five (5) Other Ranks granted leave to U/K.<br><br>One (1) Other Rank joined the Battalion. | |
| 7.10.18. | 12 (Twelve) Other Ranks granted leave to U/K. | |
| 8.10.18. | Capt. H.O.PRING and One Other Rank granted Leave to U/K. | |
| 9.10.18. | Seventy (70) Other Ranks joined the Battalion. | |
| 10.10.18. | The following Officers "Wounded" in Action.<br>CAPT. C.H.MADDIN M.C.<br>2/Lt. E.J.K.GRIMES. | |
| 9.10.18. | The following Officer "Wounded in Action"<br>CAPT. B.HOLT M.C. | |
| 10.10.18. | Five (5) Other Ranks granted leave to U/K. | |
| 14.10.18. | Twelve (12) Other Ranks granted leave to U/K.<br><br>The following Officers joined the Battalion.<br>CAPT.H.V.GOLDING.      2/Lt.E.L.CARTER.<br>2/Lt.J.L.P.ANDREWS.    2/Lt.H.SLATER.<br>2/Lt.A.C.STRIGHT.      2/Lt.H.TETT.<br>2/Lt.S.A.PAINTER. | |
| 15.10.18. | The following Officers joined the Battalion.<br>CAPT. A.T.H.BALL.    2/Lt.P.D.PARMINTER. | |
| 17.10.18. | 2/Lt.E.J.M.COOK and Five (5) Other Ranks granted leave to U/K. | |
| 15.10.18. | Thirty Five (35) Other Ranks joined the Battalion. | |

*[signature]*
Lt.Colonel.
Commanding 8th (S) Bn Somerset Light Infantry.

(Contd) PART II.

17.10.18. The Field Marshal Commanding-in-Chief under authority granted by His Majesty the King awarded the following decoration to the undernamed Officer.

### THE MILITARY CROSS.

2/Lt.L.N.Ford.        8th Som.L.I.

18.10.18. Thirteen(13) Other Ranks joined the Battalion.

19.10.18. Four(4) Other Ranks joined the Battalion.

2/Lt.D.A.HILL joined the Battalion.

18.10.18. 2/Lt.W.WOOD. joined the Battalion.

21.10.18. Five(5) Other Ranks granted Leave to U.K.

24.10.18. Five(5) Other Ranks joined the Battalion.

26.10.18. Eight(8) Other Ranks granted Leave to U.K.

29.10.18. The Field Marshal Commanding-in-Chief has, under authority granted by His Majesty the King, awarded the following decoration.

### THE DISTINGUISHED SERVICE ORDER.

Temp Capt (A/Lt.Col) C.J.de B.SHERINGHAM.M.C.
    Att.8th Somerset Light Infantry.

The Corps Commander has, under authority granted by His Majesty the King awarded the following decoration.

### THE MILITARY MEDAL.

No.235035.L/c W.J.Flower.    8th Som.L.I.Att 63rd Bde.

29.10.18. One (1) Other Rank granted Leave to U.K.

31.10.18. CAPT.W.H.GOLDING. "Killed in Action" 31.10.18.

2/LT.E.L.CARTER. "Wounded" 31.10.18.

### TOTAL CASUALTIES FOR THE MONTH.

Officers.    Killed.    1.
             Wounded.   4.

Other Ranks. Killed.    10.
             Wounded.   85.
             Missing.   1.

*Clarke Sheringham*
Lt.Colonel.
Commanding 8th.(S) Bn.Somerset Light Infy.

OPERATION ORDERS.
No.X.Z.2.
8th (S) Bn. Somerset Light Infantry.          Headquarters.

Sheet No. 51 a. 1/20,000.

1. The Battalion will carry out a raid in conjunction with the 1st Battn. N.Z.R.Brigade, on the left under cover of an Artillery and Trench Mortar bombardment.

   Troops to be employed are :- 2 platoons.
   Zero hour 03.30 hrs, 31st October.
   Watches to be synchronised at battn H.Qtrs at 23.00 hrs, 30th October.

2. Objects.
   (a) To kill and capture as many as possible of the enemy, to bring material and destroy enemy works.
   (b) To reconnoitre the ground immediately East of the Railway.

3. Plan. To enter the railway on a one platoon front, with one platoon in close support at R.35.a.40.15.
   Troops of 1st Battn N.Z.R.B. to enter railway at R.25.a.40.70.
   Platoons to move by sections in single file.
   Upon entering railway, leading platoon of 8th Somersets will work South, one section along East bank and road, One section along West bank and Road, One section in cutting along Railway, with a fourth section following in depth.
   Attached to the fourth section will be 2 R.E's.
   Attached to the section working along East bank will be 2 battalion scouts.
   The second platoon will detail :-
   (1) the leading section, to move North along railway to N.Z's and with them to mop up any of the enemy who may be occupying copse in R.35.a. West of Railway.
   (2) One L/Gun section to take up a position Commanding Southern edge of large Wood in R.35.a & b.
   (3) One section to take charge of any prisoners or assist carrying any wounded.
   (4) The 4th section will reconnoitre the ground immediately East of the Railway. The leading platoon will return to our line after proceeding some 200 yards to 300 yards south along Railway and in returning to the village all troops will avoid the Road leading from Cross-Roads to CHAPEL in X.4.b.
   D Company stretcher bearers will accompany the Raiding Party.

4. O'C "C" Company will detail one platoon to take up a position dug in from about R.34.d. central to R.34.d.6.7., this platoon will open fire on Railway and Hedge from R.35.c.22 to R.35.c.25.50, from Zero plus 4 to Zero plus 8 with the object of attracting attention of any of the enemy occupying line of Railway in R.35.c. and so enabling Raiding Party to approach along Railway from the North unobserved.

5. Stretcher Bearers of "C" Company will take up a position on sunken Road at about R.34.d.5.4. and will be prepared to assist in the evacuation of wounded.

6. "O'C "A" Company will clear all troops to West of a line drawn R.34.d.50.40. and R.34.d.60.00. until after Zero plus 4.

-- 2 --

7. **Equipment and Dress.** Fighting Order less Waterproof Sheets and Haversacks.
   Ten pairs of wire cutters per platoon to be carried, 2 bombs per man.
   Two Very Light Pistols and two packets of Very Lights per platoon.
   All letters and Military documents of any kind e.g. Maps, should be collected and left behind when Raiding Party goes out.
   An arm band of white tape will be worn on the left arm of each of the Raiding Party.

8. **Prisoners.** Prisoners will be sent direct to Battn H.Qtrs.

9. **Scouts.** Lieut H.K.Austin M.C. will detail 2 Battn Scouts to accompany the section working North along Railway.
   These Scouts will reconnoitre and report on ground immediately East of Railway, at R.34.a.80.80.

10. **Artillery etc.** Artillery, M/Guns, Stokes & 6" Newton, support as already notified.

11. **Raiding Party.** The Raiding Party will form up in assembly position immediately South of hedge at R.34.b.50.60.

12. All troops should be clear of the Railway by Zero plus 24.


Distribution.

1st Bn. N.Z.R.B.
8th Bn. Lincolnshire Regt.
O/s C. "A" "B" "C" "D" Coys.

Report on Minor Operations carried out on night of 29th/30th
October 1918 by 8th Somerset Light Infantry in conjunction
with 1st Bn.N.Z.R.B.

Reference outline of proposed raid submitted to 63rd Inf Bde
also 63rd Inf Bde Order No.271.Copy No.8.

The Artillery,Stokes and 6" Barrage opened out simultaneously
at 03.30 hrs and the advance commenced.
The two platoons under 2/Lieut E.L.CARTER and 2/Lieut D.A.HILL
respectively being formed up just South of the Copse at about
R.30.b.50.60.
Owing to the evenness of the Artillery Barrage,the Infantry were
able to close up well to the barrage getting within 12 yards of
Railway before Barrage lifted to its final line.
That the Infantry were able to get so close to the Railway is
explained by the fact that a shrapnel barrage was used bursting about
60 ft up.
Had H.E.been used the infantry could not have been so close.
On the other hand when the enemy occupies a position well dug into
the bank in a cutting it is submitted that H.E. is far more effective.
Upon reaching about R.34.b.95.10. very lights were fired in the
direction of the Raiders from a point West of the Railway about
R.35.c.15.90. and a Machine Gun opened fire simultaneously from
the hedge at about R.35.a.35.10.
This gun was firing in the direction of one platoon of "C" Coy
who had dug in at about R.34.d central at Zero minus 1½ hrs with
orders to open rapid fire at Railway between R.35.c.20.20. and
R.35.c.25.60. from Zero plus 4 to Zero plus 8.
This proved a most useful decoy as otherwise the M/Gun fire of this
and other guns would probably have been directed at the Raiding
Party.
Corporal Head in charge of No.54 Section at once got his Lewis Gun
into action and engaged the enemy M/Gun,meantime Corporal Atherton
with No.53 Section got forward into Railway through gap and opened
fire on M/Gun team from behind,killing all except one who was
badly wounded.
It is believed that this man was killed a little later by one of the
later sections.
The Lewis Gun Section then moved forward to Eastern side of Railway
and followed Corporal Atherton's section along Railway according to
programme.
Meantime Corporal Atherton and his men had overcome the opposition
of two further posts on Railway,one at R.35.c.3.8. and one at
R.35.c.25.70.
The next two sections under L/Corporal Cotton and L/Corporal Boskill
mopped up and killed several Bosches who had been missed in the
advance and were attempting to escape through hedge on Eastern side
of Railway.
When Corporal Atherton moved forward from R.35.c.25.70. he saw a
bosche M/Gunner engaging the "C" Coy platoon at R.34.d.central.
He opened fire,whereupon at once the bosche turned his gun down the
Railway,fortunately for the Raiders,firing too high.
The section was then compelled to drop and opened rapid fire,being
reinforced by a furtherv section under Corporal Head with Lewis Gun
all of whom opened fire with the result that the bosche ceased fire.
The advance was then resumed and in spite of some stick bombs being
thrown the crater was reached and the occupants killed except one
man who escaped.

Several Boches were found hiding in Bivouacs dug into the bank, and these were either shot, bayoneted or bombed.

Meantime the fifth section detailed to work Northwards having lost its section leader Corporal Rudge, (stunned by a blow and rendered unconscious) turned Southwards in error, fortunately however, 2nd Lieut D,A.HILL, realizing the mistake detailed the sixth section to work Northwards.

This section under Lance Corporal Calvert, encountered one boche at R.35.a.3,3. This man was shot, and the section then met the New Zealanders at crater R.35.a.35.40. and carried on with the reconnaisance of Triangular Orchard, New Zealanders working East side of Railway to-wards BIG WOOD.

On reaching a point about fourty yards from South Western corner, Corporal Calvert saw movement, he and his No.2. divided and approached post containing two boches who were in in the act of mounting their M/Gun to fire at remainder of lance Corporal Calverts section as they withdrew to-wards our lines. Both of these were killed, One by revolver and the other by Rifle Fire.

The 7th section went Straight to its allotted task i,e, to cover the position of the Raiding Party in centre.

On reaching gap at about R.35.a.2.1. the No.1. Private Kennel, saw three Boche by hedge on eastern side of Railway, he immediately got down and fired the L/Gun killing all three, he then advanced to position on eastern side of Railway and fired three magazines during one of which he claims to have hit 2 other Boche running across field, from about R.35.c.7.6. to-wards large wood.

The 8th section was detailed to follow with stretcher bearers and act as Prisoners escort or additional stretcher bearers.

Four Battalion Scouts were out to assist in reconnaisance and observation of enemy's position.

The hedge in front of railway is very stiff and difficult to get through, but is not exactly thick or impenetrable.

It would be well to have some gaps made by Newton 6" or Artillery fire at intervals, if a general advance through hedge is required.

No wire was met with except a thin strand and a little concertina wire in front of triangular Orchard (in slight dip in ground in front of hedge).

2 Green lights were fired from about R.35.c. central in a North Easternly Direction, also apparently one messag message - carrying Rockets, on our barrage opening.

Demolition was not required to be carried out by R.E's.

The very slight enemy artillery retalliation was most remarkable and it was noticeable the the greater part of whatever retaliation there was, was Gas and H.E. shelling on New Zealanders area, in direction of BEAUDIGNIES, at R.33.b & d.

A few 77 m.m. shells did burst West of Railway, but there did not appear to be any definite barrage line.

Our thanks are due to the 1st Bn. N.Z.R.B. for their assistance and close co-operation. To the Artillery, for their assistance and what all agreed was a most even barrage,

To the Stokes Mortars and 6" Newtons for most effective fire, and to the R.E's for sending a Sergeant and one sapper prepared to carry out demolition work.

The Raiding Party returned to our lines leaving Railway about Zero 30, 5 minutes later than scheduled.

They were unable to proceed further south than they did owing to stokes Mortar and 6" Newton block, which barraged Railway just ahead of them.

The total number of Boches killed is believed to have been between 30 and 40, and three machine Guns were destroyed.

The one prisoner taken belonged to the 83rd I.R. and upon examination at Battn H,Qtrs. stated that his Coy Strength was 50 to 60, Battn Strength about 200. That the Battn was holding

— 3 —

about a kilometres of front, that his Coy had about 450
mt metres, that he was taken about half way down his Company
front, that the right of his Company was done completely
in by the raiding party, that he had been in forward area
for four days and came from Russia, he himself being a
Saxon.

Our only casualties were:- 2nd Lieut E.L. CARTER,
(slightly wounded in the leg) and private John (wounded
in the leg and arm) not severe.

The New Zealanders killed four and captured 3 boshes,
captured 2 M/Guns and destroyed other two, and returned to
their lines without casualties.

I shall forward separate list of recommendations.

In the meantime I consider that great credit is due to
the Officers taking part, 2nd Lieut E.L. CARTER and 2nd Lieut
D.A. HILL, who lead and organised the operation most efficiently,
moving about everywhere among their platoons, and to the N.C.O's
and men taking part.

Three of the most satisfactory features of the Raid were:-
(1) The initiative and enterprise shown by section
Commanders.
(2) The fact that enemy opposition was repeatedly overcome
in the course of the operation, by the intelligent co-operation
of Riflemen and Lewis Gunners.
(3) The value of a demonstration with rapid fire from a point
well to the flank of the point opposite which raiding party
intends entering.

*[signature]*
Lt-Colonel Comdg.
1st November 1918.    8th (S) Bn. Somerset Light Infantry.

63rd Brigade.
37th Division.

8th BATTALION

THE SOMERSET LIGHT INFANTRY

NOVEMBER 1918

PART 1

## WAR DIARY.
### for
### November 1918.

| Date | Summary |
|---|---|
| 1.11.18. | The Battalion was in Brigade Support, in Billets at SALESCHES, where it stayed until the morning of the 4th. |
| 4.11.18. | See "Report on Operations" attached. |
| 5.11.18. | The Battalion marched into Billets at NEUVILLE where it stayed until the 11th. Here, most of the time was spent in cleaning up. |
| 11.11.18. | The Battalion marched into Billets at CAUDRY where it stayed until the 30th. During this period Training and various sports were carried out. |
| 12.11.18. | The Commanding Officer gave a lecture to each Company explaining the Government Scheme of Education in the Army. (a) Companies were asked to submit a roll giving the subject which each man desired to be instructed in and a meeting of representatives was arranged for the 13th. (b) List of those willing to act as instructors. |
| 13.11.18. | Meeting of Company Representatives to discuss the working of the Education Scheme. It was decided to form a Committee and that classes should be commenced. One hour out of the time allotted for training to be devoted to education each day and one hour Voluntary Classes and lectures each evening. The following Committee were elected:- |

Lt.Col.C.J.de B.SHERINGHAM D.S.O.,M.C. Commanding
2/Lt. J.MORTON.     Battalion Education Officer.
No.15173 Sgt Isaacs A.     (Battn.Hd.Qrs)
No.38313  "   Pavey W.      "B" Coy.
No.13190  "   Woodland D.   "A" Coy.
No.29232 Cpl Christopher A. "D" Coy.
No.38378 Pte Tulljames E.   "C" Coy.
No.15046 Cpl Arscott R.C.   "Transport Section".

| 15.11.18. | Capt.COLEMAN the Divisional Education Officer delivered a lecture to the Battalion on "DEMOBILIZATION & EDUCATION" This was followed with a lecture by Lt.Colonel C.J.de B.SHERINGHAM D.S.O.,M.C. Commanding, who outlined the Scheme for Education in the Battalion and as a result classes were commenced the same day. |
| 19.11.18. | Brigadier General A.B.BURBACK C.M.G. Commanding 63rd Infantry Brigade held a Brigade Ceremonial Parade Rehearsal for a Divisional Review. Companies of this Unit held various sports. |

Lt.Colonel.
Commanding 8th (S) Bn Somerset Light Infantry.

PART 1 (Contd)

20.11.18. Companies again held various sports.
The Final for the Inter-Company Football Competition was played and resulted in a win for "C" Company by 9 goals to 1.

22.11.18. The Battalion took part in a Review of the 37th Division by Major General H.B.WILLIAMS C.B., D.S.O. Commanding.

The 2nd Round of the 63rd Brigade Football Competition was played.

Result:- "C" Coy. 8th Somerset L.I......2
-- v --
63rd Brigade Hd.Qrs............1.

PROFESSOR F.J.ADKIN M.A. from G.H.Qrs. delivered the following lectures to the Battalion in the Theatre at CAUDRY.
"HOUSING, HYGIENE & EDUCATION"
26.11.18 "UNITED STATES OF AMERICA & JAPAN"

PROFESSOR ADKIN M.A. also delivered the following lectures to Battalions of the 63rd Infantry Brigade.
25.11.18. "THE SLAVS & THIER PROBLEMS"
27.11.18. "THE UNITED STATES OF AMERICA"
"GERMAN WAR AIMS"
28.11.18. "GROWTH OF GERMANY"

25.11.18. The Final of the 63rd Brigade Football Competition was played.
Result:- 4th Middlesex Regt.........2
-- v --
"C" Coy 8th Somerset L.I...0

26.11.18 The Battalion held a Cross Country Race at CAUDRY, the distance being about 3 miles. 2/Lt.ANDREWS won the race, beating the 2nd by about 100 yards.

The Battalion remained at CAUDRY until the morning of 1.12.18.

The Weather for the first half of the Month was frosty, while the remainder was the usual November weather, rain, fog, and very muddy underfoot.

*[signature]*
Lt.Colonel.
Commanding 8th (S) Bn Somerset Light Infantry

# WAR DIARY or INTELLIGENCE SUMMARY.

PART II

War diary
for
November 1918.

| Date | Summary of Events and Information |
|---|---|
| 2.11.18. | One Other Rank granted leave to U/K. |
| 3.11.18. | One Other Rank granted leave to U/K. |
| 4.11.18. | One Other Rank granted One Months' Leave to U/K. |
| 2.11.18. | Four (4) Other Ranks joined the Battalion. |
| | One hundred & thirty (130) other ranks joined the Battalion. |
| 4.11.18. | The following Officers became casualties in action.<br>Lt.a/Capt. O.BRIGGS.     "Killed"<br>2/Lt.H.W.BROOKS.         "Killed"<br>2/Lt. S.A.PALMER.        "Wounded" |
| 2.11.18. | The following Officers joined the Battalion.<br>2/Lt. D.S.LING.      2/Lt.A.C.C.DARE.<br>2/Lt.G.JACKLIN. |
| 6.11.18. | Commissions and appointments.<br>Somerset Light Infantry.<br>------------------------------<br>T/Capt. (a/Lt.Col.) C.J.de B.SHERINGHAM D.S.O.,M.C. to Command the Battalion and to be Temp.Lt.Colonel. to fill establishment 30.8.18. |
| 13.11.18. | The Corps Commander,Lt.General SIR G.M.HARPER K.C.B.,D.S.O., presented Medal Ribands to the under-named at CAUDRY.<br>THE DISTINGUISHED SERVICE ORDER.<br>Lt.Colonel C.J.de B.SHERINGHAM.<br><br>THE MILITARY CROSS.<br>Lt.Colonel C.J.de B.SHERINGHAM D.S.O.<br>Lt. H.K.AUSTIN.<br>2/Lt.L.N.FORD.<br><br>THE DISTINGUISHED CONDUCT MEDAL.<br>No. 7725 CSM. Yaw R.<br>No.15173 Sgt. Isaacs A.<br>No.30501 Pte. Pagington J.<br><br>BAR TO MILITARY MEDAL.<br>No.17091 Sgt. Chapman A.  M.M. |

*C.J.deBSheringham*
Lt.Colonel.
Commanding 8th (S) Bn Somerset Light Infantry.

## PART 11 (Contd).

**13.11.18.** Presentation of Medal Ribands Continued.

THE MILITARY MEDAL.

No. 15379 Sgt Redford F.
No. 15707 Sgt Reavley W.
No. 11640 Sgt Vaughan J.
No. 16545 Sgt Perkins A.
No. 21436 Sgt Marley J.
No. 19389 Sgt Pymont H.
No. 6892 Cpl Jackson W.G.
No. 32267 Cpl Walker W.H.
No. 26452 Cpl Moore G.
No. 26346 Cpl Baker H.
No. 27662 Cpl Millard E.
No. 40055 L/c Edwards V.
No. 265476 Pte Ford E.
No. 29806 Pte Coram W.
No. 40769 Pte Whitmore A.
No. 31138 Pte Pugh G.
No. 30046 Pte Sellick W.H.
No. 27358 Pte Bough H.
No. 49107 Pte Biggs J.

**6.11.18.** Seven (7) Other Ranks joined the Battalion.

**7.11.18.** Two (2) Other Ranks granted leave to U/K.

Four (4) Other Ranks joined the Battalion.

The following Officers joined the Battn.
2/Lt. F.H.RICHARDSON.
2/Lt. E.H.PARKES.
2/Lt. F.C.BURGESS.

LONDON GAZETTE. Extract dated 18.10.18.
Capt. C.J.PEARD D.S.O. to be Temp.Major 6.6.18.
2/Lieut. H.G.WARD to be Temp.Lieut. 13.8.18.

Capt. L.HANDLEY joined the Battalion.

**11.11.18.** Twelve (12) Other Ranks granted leave to U/K.

**9.11.18.** Thirty eight (38) Other Ranks joined the Battalion.

**13.11.18.** One (1) Other Rank granted leave to U/K.

**14.11.18.** 2/Lt.H.STONE and 2/Lt.C.C.R.PALMER granted Leave to U/K.

Lt.Colonel.
Commanding 6th (S) Bn Somerset Light Infantry.

## PART 11 (Contd).

| Date | Event |
|---|---|
| 13.11.18. | 2/Lt.D.A.MACKAY and two other ranks granted leave to PARIS. |
| 12.11.18. | Eighty five (85) Other Ranks joined the Battalion. |
| 13.11.18. | a/Capt. L.N.FORD, 2/Lt.W.J.SCOTT and twelve (12) Other Ranks granted leave to U/K. |
| 15.11.18. | Lieut. F.R.COOKSLEY M.C. joined the Battn. |
| 17.11.18. | Lieut. F.G.ADLAM joined the Battalion. Five (5) Other Ranks joined the Battn. |
| 18.11.18. | HONOURS & AWARDS. The Corps Commander, under authority granted by His Majesty the KING awarded the following decorations:- THE MILITARY MEDAL. No:28482 Sgt. Tarbox A.E. No.29826 Pte Weston C.E. |
| 20.11.18 | The following Officers joined the Battalion. Capt. H.W.POOLE (ASC)   Lt. R.LEDSHAM. 2/Lt. R.H.BUTTON. |
| 21.11.18. | Five (5) Other Ranks granted leave to U/K. Fourteen (14) Other Ranks joined the Battn. |
| 25.11.18. | Nine (9) Other Ranks joined the Battalion. |
| 23.11.18. | One Other Rank joined the Battalion. |
| 24.11.18. | Three (3) Other Ranks joined the Battalion. |
| 25.11.18. | Eleven Other Ranks joined the Battalion. Lieut. H.A.WALNE M.C. appointed Brigade Transport Officer and struck off the strength of 8th (S) Bn Somerset Light Infantry. |
| 26.11.18. | Four (4) Other Ranks granted leave to U/K. |

Lt-Colonel.
Commanding 8th (S) Bn Somerset Light Infantry.

PART II (Contd).

29.11.18.    Seven (7) Other Ranks joined the Battalion.


TOTAL CASUALTIES FOR THE MONTH.

Officers.        2      "Killed".
                 2      "Wounded".

Other Ranks.     7      "Killed"
                34      "Wounded"
                 1      "Missing".


*[signature]*
Lt.Colonel.
Commanding 6th (S) Bn Somerset Light Infantry.

Report on Operations
for November 4th & 5th 1918.

The Battalion moved off from FERME BERNIER, SALESCHES
at 06.30 hrs via X.20.b .4.8.- X.21.b.6.1.- Level Crossing
X.18.b.1.8. - Missing Cross Roads X.11.c.90.05 and
moving across country by X.17.b. and X.11d. so as to
avoid shelling, to LOUVIGNIES - RUTOY Road at about S.7.d.8.3.
thence through orchard to HAUTE RIVE FARM S.7.d.8.8. where
Battalion H.Q. remained, Companies moving on up, "A" & "B"
Coys. to just this side of RYAN de PONT a'VACHE in S.9.b.& d.
and S.3.c.

"D" Coy. to orchard in S.8.b. in touch with 10th Bn.
Royal Fusiliers, "C" Coy. to vicinity of farm CROIX ROUGE
until shelling situation made it advisable to move "C" Coy.
further forward.

All Companies passed line of LOUVIGNIES - RUTOY Rd.
between 08.10 and 08.30 hrs.

09.10 advance party sent forward to see if Battn.H.Q.
could be established at PONT a'VACHE; No word being received
by 10.00. I went forward, on the way instructing "C" Coy. at
CROIX ROUGE to move forward. Shelling of S.8.b.& c.
S.9.a.& c. heavy, found "D" Coy. and told them to push
forward patrols and to establish touch with 15th Bn. Royal
Fusiliers on flanks. I then found "A" & "B" Coys. in
valley of RYAN de PONT a'VACHE and learned that
O.C. "A" Coy. had been killed.

Enemy sniping and Machine Gun fire was most active
from orchard S.W. of JOLIMETZ and movement down into valley
was difficult. I could not find O.C. "B" Coy. but learnt
shortly afterwards that he must have been killed almost while
I was visiting the companies in front line.
Both these two company commanders lost their lives in
reconnoitring forward with a view to merging with
1st/1st Herts Regt. in order to make a further attack.

At 13.00 hrs I ordered Companies to push out patrols
and keep close touch with the enemy with a view to further
advance. At 14.00 hrs I ordered two leading companies
to push forward in conjunction with 1st/1st Herts as soon
as possible.

Shortly after, report received that the Boche had retired.
Companies were immediately ordered (14.20 hrs) to push
right on to JOLIMETZ and beyond.

15.40 hrs, Support Coy. (with H.Q at S.11.b.85.30)
reports being in touch with right Coy.; with Reserve Coy.
close up. I found the best part of my leading Coys. on main
road in S.11.a., took them forward and started them through
wood.

Report timed 17.00 hrs from Left Coy. that they were well
into wood in S.6.d. but meeting with Heavy Machine Gun fire
on right flank, touch lost with "B" Coy.

At 16.40 hrs Left Coy. reported touch with 15th Royal
Fusiliers at T.7.b.3.2. but reported not able to get on
owing to thickness of undergrowth.
The left Coy. encountered 3 enemy machine guns and a sniper
at about T.1.c.45.25 and T.1.c.15.50 at about 17.20 hrs.

They opened fire with rifles and Lewis Gun on the
enemy who was seen to withdraw carrying one of their
number who was apparently wounded, we had two casualties one
killed and one slightly wounded. The enemy were followed up
but owing to the thickness of the wood and our ignorance of
the way they were not found.

A similar experience was met with by "B" Coy. further South, one enemy machine gun with four men being encountered which withdrew on fire being opened on the enemy - the party escaped in the darkness.

Decided to push Support and Reserve Companies through along main rides with strong platoon patrols supported by a second platoon.

Ordered "D" Coy. to send patrols down road and railway South Eastwards from T.7.b.25.20 and T.7.b.40.25 respectively to T.8.d.10.00 and T.8.d.05.35, and "C" Coy. to T.8.c.60.25 and thence to T.8.b.95.00 and T.8.c.60.20. each patrol to establish strong posts at these points if possible and then push on to reconnoitre eastern exits of wood. Moved to forward report centre at T.7.b.35.80 where I found two Company Commanders 13th Royal Fusiliers.

Later established line of posts T.8.c.80.30. - T.8.b.95.05.- T.8.d.05.85 - T.8.d.10.00 with protective listening posts connecting same up.

Three Officer patrols went out one to a point on Railway 50 to 100 yards from eastern exits from wood. Several fires were observed and from 15 to 20 of the enemy were seen passing in front of these fires. A patrol proceeding from T.8.c.60.30 towards T.3.a.80.50, saw 10 of the enemy at this point. Another patrol going from T.8.c.60.30 towards T.8.c.40.70 saw two of the enemy at this point.

Reported situation to Brigade by telephone from T.7.b.35.80.

In this connection I wish to report that the Battn. Signallers laid and maintained lines from T.12.b.80.75 (JOLIMONT) to T.7.b.35.75.

In the morning learning that 5th Division intended using main drives and railways through wood I ordered Coys. to establish posts at eastern exits so as to deny the observation along drives and railways to enemy.

The leading battalions of the 5th Division on arrival between 03.30 and 04.30 hrs were not aware that we had reached far edge of wood and were intending forming up on western edge of wood in attack formations.

I informed them at once of our position and urged them to shove on down rides to eastern edge of wood. Their Battalions passed through our troops and across eastern edge of wood between 06.30 hrs and 06.40 hrs.

They reported taking prisoners, 1 officer and 8 other ranks in vicinity of T.7.a.80.50.

Between 07.30 and 08.00 leading Battalions of 5th Division reported having gone through our leading troops and having passed THE DOTTED LINE, the telephone line being dies and no instructions having been received we were unable to withdraw, between 10.30 and 11.00 when we received instructions from you that we might withdraw.

We at once moved to PONT a' VACHE where we met the cookers at about 12.00 and where breakfast was taken.

The Battalion then marched by companies via LOUVIGNIES and SALESCHES to billets in BEAUVILLE, reaching BEAUVILLE between 15.30. & 16.00hrs.

Enemy's Guns captured during this tour in the line being:-

1. 5.9" Howitzer.
20. Machine Guns.

I have to report the following casualties:-

Lt. A/Capt.   C.BRIGGS.     "Killed"    4.11.18.
2.Lt.         H.F.BROOKS.    do          do
2/Lt.         S.A.PALMER.   "Wounded"    do.

Other ranks:

"Killed"                5.
"Wounded"              22.
"Missing
 believed wounded."     3.

                                    *signature*
                                        Lt.Colonel.
8.11.18.    Commanding 6th (S) Bn. Somerset Light Infantry.

5th November 1918.

My Dear Sheringham.

I want to convey my best thanks to you and your Battalion for the splendid way you helped us out yesterday, I thought at one time that things were not going to p an out very well on the right owing to the Hertfordshire Regiment having lost the barrage. This was due to the Essex Regt, being held up at one post by a Machine Gun nest round the Chapel by the Railway which had not been mopped up, making them an hour late at the Blue Dotted Line and leaving the Herts flank exposed to M.G. fire from N. part of JOLIMETZ.

However all's well that ends well and we gave the Boche a hell of a doing.

It was splendid the way your fellows pushed through in the afternoon and got to their objective.

Yours sincerely,

W.L. HERBERT.

63rd Brigade.
37th Division.

8th BATTALION

THE SOMERSET LIGHT INFANTRY

DECEMBER 1918

PART 1

## WAR DIARY
### for
### DECEMBER 1918.

**1.12.18.**  The Battalion marched from CAUDRY to HAUSSY and was billeted there for one night.

**2.12.18.**  The Battalion marched to ORSINVAL where it stayed until the 13th.

**3.12.18 to 13.12.18.**  Education, Training, Sports, Inter-platoon Football matches, were carried out.

**6.12.18.**  "B" & "C" Coys of this Unit challenged each other to any kind of sport.
Both Companies turned out in strength, dressed in various costumes, each Company having its own tin Band. The affair was a great success, causing much fun & amusement which was greatly appreciated by the Troops.
"B" Coy obtained the most points and won the day.

**8.12.18.**  The Battalion played the 1st Bn Somerset L.I. at Football. The match was played at CURGIES before many spectators of each Battalion.
Result:-
  8th Bn. Somerset L.I. ------1
  1st Bn Somerset L.I. ------0

**11.12.18.**  The Regimental Concert Party known as the "Pip-Acks" gave two Concerts at ORSINVAL.
One Concert was given to "A" & "B" Coys and the other to "C" & "D" Coys. It was a great success.

**12.12.18.**  The "Pip-Acks" gave another concert for the benefit of Battalion HdQrs and the Transport Section.

**13.12.18.**  The Battalion marched into Billets at St. WAAST where it stayed for one night.

**14.12.18.**  The Battalion marched to SOUS-LE-BOIS staying for two nights.

**16.12.18**  The Battalion marched into Billets at GRAND RENG and were reviewed on the march by the Corps Commander LIEUT.GENERAL SIR G.M.HARPER K.C.B.,D.S.O. who expressed his satisfaction. The Battalion stayed at GRAND RENG for one night.

**17.12.18.**  The Battalion moved to BINCHE where it was Billeted for one night.

**18.12.18**  The Battalion marched into Billets at COURCELLES where it stayed for one night.

*[signature]*
Lt. Colonel.
Commanding 8th (S) Bn Somerset Light Infantry.

## PART 1 (Contd).

marched
19.12.18. The Battalion/to FRASNES-LES-GOSSELIES in the pouring rain. Everybody was soaked to the skin on their arrival. The inhabitants gave the Battalion a hearty welcome and did all in their power to dry the Troop's clothes and make them all comfortable. The whole Battalion have excellent Billets.

22.12.18. The First batch of Coal-Miners were sent home to be demobilized, 16 in number.

25.12.18. Christmas Day. The ground covered with snow. The Battalion had an excellent Christmas Dinner which was followed by Company Concerts.

26.12.18.
to 31.12.18. Education, Training, Sports Etc were carried out daily.

The weather for the month was very wet and trying.

The following is a copy of a letter issued by 37th Divisional Headquarters dated 26.12.18.

"The Divisional Commander wishes to congratulate all ranks on the very fine performance of the Division on its advance into BELGIUM.

"The advance entailed 6 days marching over bad roads and in inclement weather, and covered an average distance of 54 miles.

"The Staff arrangements for of formations were good. The attention paid to march discipline by Commanding Officers resulted in the marches being accomplished with the least amount of discomfort to the troops. The small wastage reflected the greatest credit on the standard of man-mastership prevailing in all dismounted formations and Units.

"The spirit of the troops was excellent, and the keeness displayed by them must have given them as much satisfaction as it did to all those who had the privilege of seeing them on the march".

Capt. YATES (A.V.C) delivered a lecture at ORSINVAL on "CARE OF HORSES" 13.12.18.

### EDUCATION.

A Competition was arranged for the best ESSAY on "THE GOVERNMENT EDUCATION SCHEME". The maximum number of points was 100 and small prizes were offered. The result was published on 15.12.18 as follows.
1. No. 50421 L/c Young A. 90 points.
2. No. 29784 Cpl Atherton. 85 "
3. No. 54540 Pte Neville. 80 "

Lt. Colonel.
Commanding 8th (S) Bn Somerset Light Infantry.

PART 1

WAR DIARY
for
December 1918.

8th (S) Bn Somerset L.I.

9.12.18. The following is an Extract from the "Times" dated 9.12.18.

SERVICE BATTALION FLAGS.

Substitutes for the KING'S Colour.

   A proposal to present colours to the 8th Somerset Light Infantry to be used by them when they march into Germany cannot be carried into effect. The Colours were to have been presented by relatives residing in BATH of men of the Somersets who have fallen in the War. In a letter to Sir HARRY HATT, the Army Council state that owing to difficulties and especially the delay that would be entailed by manufacture it has been decided that Colours as prescribed for infantry battalions cannot be provided for service battalions raised solely for service during the war. For the purposes of ceremonials in France the KING has approved of the presentation of silk Union Flags to Service Battalions to be used as substitutes for the KING'S Colour. These flags are in course of manufacture and will probably be sent this week to France, where they will be consecrated and handed to those Battalions that are not in possession of Colours.
   The communication concludes:- You will no doubt recognize that the Council could not accord preferential treatment to any particular Battalion by allowing it to receive colours from private sources while many other battalions in similar circumstances would not be fortunate enough to receive presentations of the nature so generously put forward by you in the case of the 8th Battalion Somerset Light Infantry.

## PART 11

| | |
|---|---|
| 2.12.18. | Major E.C. CARTWRIGHT M.C. and nine (9) Other Ranks granted leave to U/K. |
| 5.12.18. | 4 Other Ranks granted leave to U/K. |
| | 14 (fourteen) Other Ranks joined the Battalion. |
| 12.12.18. | 10 (ten) Other Ranks joined the Battalion. |
| 9.12.18. | 9 (nine) Other Ranks granted leave to U/K. |
| 11.12.18. | 2 (two) Other Ranks granted leave to U/K. |
| 13.12.18. | 4 (four) Other Ranks granted leave to U/K. |
| 12.12.18. | 2 Other Ranks granted leave in France. |
| 8.12.18. | APPOINTMENTS & COMMISSIONS. The following extract from List No.217 appointments, commissions etc-, dated 8.12.18 approved by the Field Marshal Commanding-in-Chief the British Armies in France. 8th (S) Bn Somerset L.I. Temp.Major C.J.PEARD D.S.O. (Capt.S.R.) to be 2nd-in-Command to fill establishment 1.11.18. |
| 16.12.18. | His Majesty the KING has awarded the following decorations. THE MILITARY CROSS. 2 Lt.E.L.CARTER.      8th Som.L.I. Distinguished Conduct Medal. No.29684 Cpl Atherton W.J.R.    8th Som.L.I. |
| 16.12.18. | 9 (nine) Other Ranks granted leave to U/K. |
| 20.12.18. | 4 (four) Other Ranks granted leave to U/K. |
| 23.12.18. | 27 (twenty seven) Other Ranks granted leave to U/K. |
| 14.12.18. | No.10218 R.S.M. GALOSKA J. proceeded to 2nd Army Headquarters Intelligence Department. |
| 22.12.18. | 16 (sixteen) Other Ranks proceeded to England for demobilization as Coalminers. |
| 26.12.18. | 8 (eight) Other Ranks proceeded to U/K on Leave. |
| 24.12.18. | 45 (forty five) Other Ranks proceeded to England for demobilization as Coalminers. |
| 25.12.18. | 8 (eight) Other Ranks proceeded to England for demobilization as Coal miners. |
| 23.12.18. | 12 (twelve) Other Ranks proceeded to Eng. for demobilization as Coal Miners. |

*[signature]*
Lt. Colonel.
Commanding 8th (S) Bn Somerset Light Infantry.

PART 11 (contd).

26.12.18. Two Other Ranks proceeded to England for demobilization.

24.12.18. No.7725 C.S.M.YAW R. appointed Acting Regimental Sergeant Major.

*[signature]*
Lt.Colonel.
Commanding 8th (S) Bn Somerset Light Infantry.

# WAR DIARY
## for
## JANUARY 1919.

### PART I

**1.1.19 to 31.1.19.**
    The Battalion was billeted in FRASNES - LES - COSSELIES. During this period Training, various Sports etc. were carried out.
    Every monday small parties of men visited BRUSSELS. The parties were conveyed to BRUSSELS in by Motor Lorries on Monday morning, returning in Lorries on Tuesday night.

**13.1.19.** A Dinner was given by the Sergeants of this Unit, to which the Commanding Officer, Adjutant, Company Commanders, Quartermaster, & Transport Officer were invited. The Dinner was followed with a Concert by the Regimental Concert Party, and after the Concert a Dance. A very enjoyable evening was spent, and the whole show was a great success.

**17.1.19.** A Dinner, similar to that given by the Sergeants was given to the Regimental Band. This was also a great success.

**16.1.19.** A lecture was delivered by Mr. HATZFIELD in the Y.M.C.A. FRASNES. Subject. "ROUND THE WORLD IN WARTIME". 150 Other Ranks of this Unit attended.

**20.1.19.** A trip to WATERLOO was arranged. The party was conveyed to WATERLOO in Motor Lorries, returning the same day.

**21.1.19.** Lt.Col. APLIN D.S.O. from the War Office lectured to this Battalion on "DEMOBILIZATION & RECONSTRUCTION". It was an excellent lecture and was very much appreciated by the men.

    Several Football Matches in the Division League were played. Owing to the demobilization, in almost every match a different team was chosen to represent this Battalion with a result that each match was lost.

    The weather for the month was very cold, the ground being covered with snow for three parts of January.

*G.B. Sheringham*
Lt. Colonel.
Commanding 8th (s) Bn Somerset Light Infantry.

WAR DIARY
for
JANUARY 1919.

PART II

1.1.19.  MAJOR C.J.PEARD D.S.O. joined the Battalion.

3.1.19.  R.S.M.SYKES and 8 Other Ranks joined the Battalion.

5.1.19.  2/Lt.J.H.LUGG and 16 Other Ranks granted leave to U/K.

MENTIONS IN DESPATCHES.
T/Lt.Col.J.H.M.HARDYMAN D.S.O.,M.C. (Killed).
Major C.J.Peard D.S.O.
T/Capt.H.O.Pring.
T/2nd Lt.R.Erskine.
2/Lt.H.M.Eyres.

No.3340 Sgt.Bglr. J.Calver.

The above are extracts from Supplements to the London Gazette dated 27.12.18.

3.1.19.  2/Lt.L.M.CREES joined the Battalion.

27.12.18.  2/Lt.D.A.MACKEY granted leave to U/K.

6.1.19.  MAJOR E.C.CARTWRIGHT M.C. granted "Special Leave to U/K.

9.1.19.  HONOURS & AWARDS. The Field Marshall Commanding-in-Chief, under authority granted by His Majesty the KING awarded the following decorations to the undernamed.

BAR TO THE MILITARY CROSS.

T/Capt.C.H.MADDEN-M-C-   8th Som.L.I.

THE MILITARY CROSS.

2/Lt.W.H.BROOKS. 8th Som.L.I. (Killed).

THE DISTINGUISHED CONDUCT MEDAL.

No.27822 Pte H.MUDDLE. 8th Som.L.I.

10.1.19.  9 (Nine) Other Ranks granted leave to U/K.

17 (Seventeen) Other Ranks joined the Battalion.

9.1.19.  The following Officers proceeded to U/K to be Demobilized.
CAPT-P.H.R.BENNETT.      Lt.L.C.BODLEY.
2/Lt.W.WOOD.             Lt.F.G.ADLAM.
MAJOR E.C.CARTWRIGHT-M.C. (on leave).

## PART II Contd.

| Date | Summary of Events and Information |
|---|---|
| 9.1.19. | 24 (Twenty four) Other Ranks to U/K to be demobilized. |
| | Capt. A.K.M.BALL and One Other Rank attached to Locomotive Works, St.ETIENNE, struck off the strength 8th Som.L.I. |
| 11.1.19. | 3 (Three) Other Ranks proceeded to U/K to be demobilized. |
| 14.1.19. | 27 (Twenty seven) Other Ranks granted Leave to U/K. |
| 17.1.19. | 10 (ten) Other Ranks granted leave to U/K. |
| 18.1.19. | 2/Lt.E.H.PARKES and 43 (Forty Three) Other ranks proceeded to U/K for demobilization. |
| 20.1.19. | 2/Lt.L.J.P.ANDREWS and 37 (Thirty seven) Other Ranks proceeded to U/K to be demobilized. |
| 19.1.19. | One Other Rank granted "Special" Leave to U/K. |
| 20.1.19. | Capt. L.HANDLEY granted "Special" Leave to U/K. |
| 21.1.19. | 10 (ten) Other Ranks granted leave to U/K. |
| 22.1.19. | One Other Rank granted "King's Leave" to U/K. |
| | 12 (Twelve) Other Ranks proceeded to U/K to be demobilized. |
| 21.1.19. | 2/Lt.L.P.B.DOMAN and 5 (Five) Other Ranks granted leave to U/K. |
| 25.1.19. | 36 (Thirty Six) Other Ranks proceeded to U/K for demobilization. |
| 28.1.19. | 10 (ten) Other Ranks granted leave to U/K. |
| 26.1.19. | 15 (Fifteen) Other Ranks proceeded to U/K to be demobilized. |
| 27.1.19. | The KING has been pleased to approve of the following award to the undernamed. |
| | **MERITORIOUS SERVICE MEDAL.** |
| | No.15107 RQMS- DOE.P.M.M.   8th Som.L.I. |
| | No.17416 Sgt.A.HALL.         8th Som.L.I. |
| | 29 (Twenty nine) Other Ranks proceeded to U/K to be demobilized. |
| 30.1.19. | 2/Lt.H.TETT and 42 (Forty two) Other Ranks proceeded to U/K for demobilization. |

Lt.Colonel.
Commanding 8th Somerset Light Infantry.

PART I

WAR DIARY for
FEBRUARY 1919.

| Date | |
|---|---|
| 1.2.19. | The Battalion was still in Billets at FRASNES-LES-GOSSELIES. We had snow during the day, and it was very cold. |
| 2.2.19. | Snowing best part of the day. |
| 3.2.19. | The Corps Commander, Lt.General Sir.G.M.HARPER KCB,DSO. presented this Battalion with the UNION COLOURS. Lt.H.H.AUSTIN M.C. received the Colours. This ceremony was performed at FRASNES-les-GOSSELIES. The ground was covered with snow. |
| 5.2.19. | Lt.Commander EVERARD gave a lecture on "THE WORK of the NAVY". It snowed again on this day. |
| 6.2.19. | Rifleman J.DILLSEN gave a lecture on "ENGLISH as she is SPOKEN". From the 6th to the 11th the weather was very cold and ground covered with snow. |
| 11.2.19. | Brigadier General A.B.HUBBACK CMG,DSO lectured on "THE MALAY PENINSULA". From the 12th to 18th weather very dull. 18th raining all the afternoon. 19 & 20th weather fine. |
| 21.2.19. | Brigadier General A.B.HUBBACK CMG,DSO. lectured to the Officers of the 63rd Infantry Brigade on "WATERLOO". All Officers of this Battalion attended. |
| 22.2.19 to 28.2.19. | The weather was fine. All kinds of sports were carried out during the month, including a Battalion Boxing Competition, and the final for the Battalion Football Competition which was won by "B" Coy. |

*[signature]*
Lt.Colonel.
Commanding 8th (S) Bn Somerset Light Infantry.

# WAR DIARY or INTELLIGENCE SUMMARY

## PART II

| Date | Summary of Events and Information |
|---|---|
| 4.2.19. | 2/Lt.T.E.DAVEY and 11 Other Ranks granted leave to U/K. |
| | 5 Other Ranks despatched to U/K for Demobilization. |
| 5.2.19. | 17 Other Ranks proceeded to U/K for Demobilization. |
| 7.2.19. | 7 Other Ranks granted leave to U/K. |
| 8.2.19. | 17 Other Ranks to U/K demobilized. |
| 9.2.19. | 16 Other Ranks to U/K demobilized. |
| 10.2.19. | The Divisional Commander, Major General. C.B.WILLIAMS CB,DSO, presented medal ribbands to the following Other Ranks of this Battalion at FRASNES-LES-GOSSELIES. |

No.18292 Sgt.Durman W.        D.C.M.
No.27082 Cpl Huddle H.         M.M.
No.44480 Sgt Drowan A.         M.M.
No.28482 Sgt Tarbox.A.         M.M.
No.11633 Pte Rowles J.E.       M.M.
No.28467 Cpl Smart G.          M.M.
No.15107.RQMS.P.M.Doe.         M.S.M.

| | |
|---|---|
| 11.2.19. | 15 Other Ranks granted Leave to U/K. |
| 12.2.19. | Lt.R.LEDSHAM and 30 Other Ranks to U/K demobilized. |
| 14.2.19. | 5 Other Ranks to U/K demobilized. Capt. L.HANDLEY to U/K demobilized. |
| 18.2.19. | 7 Other Ranks granted leave to U/K. |
| 19.2.19. | 5 Other Ranks to U/K demobilized. |
| 21.2.19. | 7 Other Ranks granted Leave to U/K. Capt.D.A.HILL granted leave to U/K. |
| 22.2.19. | 2 Other Ranks to U/K demobilized. |
| 25.2.19. | 6 Other Ranks to U/K on leave. |
| 27.2.19. | The following extract from List.No.827 d/- 10.2.19 Appointments, Commissions Etc, approved by the Field Marshal Commanding - In - Chief, the British Armies in France. 8th Som.L.I. T/Lt.F.R.COOKSLEY M.C. to be Acting Captain whilst Commanding a Company 24.1.19. |

Geo D Cunningham
Lt.Colonel,
Commanding 8th (S) Bn Somerset Light Infantry.

Lt.Col. Sir Frederick Ponsonby Bart.

    St James Palace.

        London W.

Sir,
        In confirmation of our conversation over telephone on 22nd and on behalf of 8th (S) Bn. Lincolnshire Regt. and 8th (S) Bn. Somerset L.I. I should be most grateful if you could ask HIS MAJESTY THE KING if He would feel disposed so far to interest Himself in a project we have in hand as to speak to the Dean of WESTMINSTER in connection with it.

        The project is this.-
        The late Revd. T.B.HARDY C.C., D.S.O., M.C. was Padre with the two Battalions throughout the campaign until being wounded in action in October 1918.

        His gallantry, modesty and Christianity were known to and admired by all ranks.

        He is looked upon by all in the two battalions as indeed a National Hero. He earned his decorations many times over by countless unrecorded acts of bravery and when his death was made known from his wound in October both battalions were greatly moved.

        A sum of £50. was immediately subscribed in one battalion and a collection is to be made in the other. I have very little doubt that a very much larger sum will eventually be subscribed if necessary as there are many who were not with the battalions at the time, and many relatives of those serving at one time or another who will wish to share in the erection of a memorial.

        It occured to us that there is no better place for such a memorial than WESTMINSTER ABBEY or ST PAUL's in either of which places so many national heroes have been commemorated.

        It also struck us that as HIS MAJESTY knew the Padre personally, and had so far honoured him as to appoint him one of His Chaplains, and that as the Padre is probably the only Padre in the present war who has had the distinction of being granted all three service decorations, HIS MAJESTY might be interested in asking the Dean of WESTMINSTER on our behalf whether there is a suitable corner for such a memorial.

        yours very truly

        (Sd) C.J.de.B.SHERINHAM.

        Lieut-Colonel.
3/2/19.   Commanding 8th (S) Bn. Somerset Light Infantry.

PART II.

## WAR DIARY.
### for the month of March 1919.

| Place | Date | Hour | Summary of Events and Information | Remarks |
|---|---|---|---|---|
| | 2/3/19. | | 9 Other Ranks granted leave to U/K for 4/3/19 - 18/3/19. | |
| | | | 21 O.R.'s despatched to U/K for demobilization 3 O.R.'s Re-enlisted proceeded to U/K for furlough. | |
| | | | Lt.Col.C.J.de H.Sheringham to U/K for duty A.M.S. 1604 4th Army d/-28/2/19. | |
| | 3/3/19. | | The Army Commander has awarded the following decoration to the undernamed. (Authy:.4thArmy No.HR/220 3/MS d/-18/2/19. | |
| | | | THE MILITARY MEDAL. | |
| | | | No. 15083 CQMS ARSCOTT H. 8th Somerset L.I. | |
| | | | 6 Other Ranks demobilized while on leave in the U/K. | |
| | 4/3/19. | | Major Bt Lt.Col. E.C.L. WORTHINGTON-WILMER joined the Battalion for attachment. | |
| | | | Major Bt Lt.Col. E.C.L. WORTHINGTON WILMER evacuated to No 55 C.C.S. | |
| | | | 2 O.R.'s granted leave to the U/K for 28/2/19 - 14/3/19. | |
| | | | The following Officers granted leave to the U/K.<br>2/Lt B.S.LING.<br>2/Lt A.C.C.DARE.<br>2/Lt F.H.RICHARDSON. | |
| | 5/3/19. | | 4 O.R.'s granted leave to the U/K for 7/3/19 - 21/3/19. | |
| | 6/3/19. | | A/Capt G.JACKLIN granted leave to the U/K. | |
| | 7/3/19. | | 2/Lt F.C.BURGESS granted leave to the U/K. | |
| | 9/3/19. | | 6 O.R.'s granted leave to the U/K for 11/3/19 - 25/3/19. | |
| | | | A/Capt F.R.COOKSLEY.M.C. granted leave to the U/K. | |
| | | | 2/Lt B.S.LING proceeded to join the 151 Chinese Labour Coy. | |
| | | | 2/Lt J.H.LUGG proceeded to join the 136 Chinese Labour Coy. | |
| | | | 2/Lt C.C.R.PALMER proceeded to join the 136 Chinese Labour Coy. | |

C.J.Peard.
Lieut.Colonel.
Commanding 8th(S) Bn Somerset Light Infantry.

PART 11 Contd.

| Date | Summary of Events and Information |
|---|---|
| 13/3/19. | 2/Lt. F.C. BURGESS proceeded to join the 33rd Chinese Labour Coy. |
| | 13.O.R.'s granted leave to the U/K for 13/3/19 - 27/3/19. |
| 14/3/19. | The undernamed Officers demobilized on the dates shown against their names. Lt. W.E. BYWATER. 23/2/19. Lt. T.J.M. COOK. do. Lt. N.H. CREES. 19/2/19. (Authy:-Part 11 Base Orders No 19 d/-8/3/19 |
| 15/3/19. | 18.O.R.'s despatched to the U/K for demobilization, 7 O.R.'s Re-enlisted proceeded to U/K for furlough. |
| | 2/Lt A.C.C. DARE proceeded to U/K (Repatriation). |
| | 2/Lt H. STONE granted leave to the U/K. |
| | 3.O.R.'s granted leave to the U/K for 16/3/19 - 30/3/19. |
| 16/3/19. | Capt. H.A. WALNE. M.C. joined the battalion. |
| | Capt. H.A. WALNE. M.C. granted leave to U/K. |
| 19/3/19. | Lt. W.K. AUSTIN. M.C. granted leave to U/K. |
| | 5.O.R.'s granted leave to U/K for 20/3/19 - 3/4/19. |
| 22/3/19. | 8.O.R.'s granted leave to U/K for 23/3/19 - 6/4/19. |
| | Capt D.J.L. ROUTH to U/K demobilized |
| 24/3/19. | No. 7725. C.S.M. Yaw appointed A/R.S.M. |
| | 2/Lt. E. PFAFF. to U/K demobilized. |
| 26/3/19. | 9.O.R.'s granted leave to the U/K |
| 27/3/19. | 2.O.R.'s despatched to the U/K for demobilization. 2.O.R.'s Re-enlisted proceeded to U/K for furlough. |
| 31/3/19. | 15.O.R.'s demobilized while on leave in the U/K. |

C.J. Peard.
Lieut. Colonel.
Commanding 8th(S) Bn. Somerset Light Infantry.

# WAR DIARY or INTELLIGENCE SUMMARY

PART 1.

WAR DIARY for
MARCH 1919.

| Place | Date | Hour | Summary of Events and Information | Remarks |
|---|---|---|---|---|
| | 11/3/19. | | The battalion vacated Billets at FRASNES-LES-GOSSELIES and marched into billets at JUMET, route Via GOSSELIES leaving FRASNES-LES-GOSSELIES at 10.am and arriving at JUMET at 12.30.pm. | |
| | | | Demobilization was carried on in small parties during the month. | |
| | | | Leave was given freely to Officers and Other Ranks with 3 & 7 months duration respectively. | |

C.J.Peard.
Lieut.Colonel.
Commanding 8th(S) Bn Somerset Light Infantry.

PART I.

WAR DIARY.
for the month of April 1919.

| | |
|---|---|
| 1/4/19. | Battalion in Billets in JUMET (BELGIUM) |
| 14/4/19. | The CADRE of the 8th (S) Bn. Somerset Light Infantry 5 Officers and 46 Other Ranks, also equipment and Transport less Animals entrained at CHARLEROI for ANTWERP en route for GLENCORSE Scotland, leaving CHARLEROI at 7.p.m. 14/4/19. |
| 15/4/19. | Arrived at ANTWERP and Camped at No. 2 Embarkation Camp, awaiting instructions for Embarkation. |
| 17/4/19. | The Battalion with equipment and Transport Embarked at 4.p.m. on "H.M.T.S. AJAX". |
| 18/4/19. | 6.a.m. "H.M.T.S. AJAX" proceeded to SOUTHAMPTON, arriving 9.30.a.m. 20/4/19. |
| 20/4/19. | The Battalion stores and vehicles unloaded and entrained at SOUTHAMPTON and proceeded at 6.30 p.m. to GLENCORSE Scotland via Winchester, Banbury, York, Durham, Newcastle, and Berwick, arriving at GLENCORSE at 6.p.m. 21/4/19. |
| 22/4/19. | 1 Officer and 34 Other Ranks proceeded to their respective Dispersals Areas for Demobilization. |
| 26/4/19. | The following Officers and Other Ranks proceeded with the Colours of the 8th (S) Bn. Somerset Light Infantry to the Regimental Depot at TAUNTON. |

| | | |
|---|---|---|
| Lieut.Col. | C.J.PEARD. | D.S.O. |
| Capt. | H.O.PRING. | |
| Lieut. | D.G.CAMPBELL. | |
| Lieut. | H.K.AUSTIN. | M.C. |

| | | |
|---|---|---|
| 15107. | RQMS. | Doe P.M.M. |
| 9275. | CQMS. | Perry R. |
| 16001. | Sgt. | Somerton R.O. |
| 15206. | Sgt. | Prout T. |
| 15429. | Cpl. | Moses C.S. |
| 21695. | L/c. | Haggett G. |
| 12153. | Pte. | Vines A.H. |
| 30021. | Pte. | Hornsby H.W. |
| 16061. | Pte. | Appleton F. |
| 20995. | Pte. | Reed J.E. |
| 28296. | Pte. | Crowhurst E.G. |
| 29978. | Pte. | Castle R.F. |

Lieut. Colonel
Commanding 8th (S) Bn. Somerset Light Infantry.

www.ingramcontent.com/pod-product-compliance
Lightning Source LLC
Chambersburg PA
CBHW081527160426
43191CB00011B/1697